Generational Change and Social Policy Challenges

Australia and South Korea

Edited by Ruth Phillips

SYDNEY UNIVERSITY PRESS

Published by

SYDNEY UNIVERSITY PRESS

University of Sydney Library

www.sup.usyd.edu.au

Sydney University Press

Fisher Library F03

University of Sydney

NSW 2006 AUSTRALIA

Email: info@sup.usyd.edu.au

ISBN 978-1-920898-64-9

Individual papers are available electronically through the Sydney eScholarship Repository at:

http://ses.library.usyd.edu.au/handle/2123/1966

Cover design and print by University Publishing Service, the University of Sydney.

Contents

Foreword

For a century or more, Australians have been interested in how our social and economic trends stand up against other nations. Such comparisons have helped us to identify bragging rights when things here are done particularly well, to show us where our performance is not good when compared with what is being achieved abroad, and to highlight what new issues and policies we ought to be thinking about.

Over that century, of course, the international comparisons of Australia's performance were mostly made against the other English-speaking countries with which, to varying degrees, we shared a common history – notably the United Kingdom, Canada, New Zealand and the United States.

A quantum jump in the range of countries that became comparable to Australia took place over the late 1970s and the 1980s, when the Organisation for Economic Cooperation and Development (OECD) first established a body of readily accessible information on a wide variety of social and economic trends in its member states. As a result, it became more feasible to show how Australia measured up against the rich countries of continental Europe, North America and Japan. Korea joined the OECD in 1996; however, there were long delays in the incorporation of Korean material into OECD data and studies.

Over recent years, a number of studies have tapped into the rich vein of what can be learned from a detailed analysis of how Australia's experience and trends look when compared with what is happening in one or more countries in Asia. It is inevitable that we will see many more Asian-Australian comparative studies over coming years and there is little doubt that they will be of great value to Australians; Australia is increasingly linked with Asian countries in trade, regional strategic interests and the exchange of people. More importantly, the social and economic variety of societies and policies across Asia provides great opportunity for study and comparison and change in Asia is happening at a breathtaking pace.

The conference on generational change, hosted by the University of Sydney–based Research Institute for Asia and the Pacific in November 2005, is an outstanding example of the fresh insights achieved when experts from an Asian country and Australia are brought together to consider a topical issue. The focus of the conference was the nature and implications of generational change in Australia and Korea, with a strong emphasis on looking forward and suggesting important policy responses to key generational change problems.

Korea and Australia have much in common: on a global scale both are mid-sized economies; both are experiencing rapid change; both have large middle classes; both put a high value on education; and both populations are quick to adopt new technologies. At the same time, there are key differences. For example, demographic change is more rapid in Korea; Korea has a particularly powerful network for broadband; and compared with Korea the Australian workforce has a substantial build up of funded assets in superannuation (pension funds).

The Australia-Korea Foundation, which is, in itself, reflective of the important relationship between the two countries, provided financial support for this conference. The Foundation was established in 1992, and is funded by the Australian Government, to broaden and to strengthen the relationship between Australia and Korea. On behalf of the Board of the Australia-Korea Foundation, I thank the Australian and Korean researchers who participated in the conference on generational change, and I congratulate The Research Institute for Asia and the Pacific on its initiative and achievement supporting the development and publication of this book.

Don Stammer

Chairman
Australia-Korea Foundation

1

Diverse histories, shared social issues: the Australian and Korean welfare states

Ruth Phillips

Introduction

As recognised by social policy scholars, social policy in Korea[1] is a relatively new field of governance and practice (Chang-sik & Shaw, 2003; Huck-Ju, 1997; Sung, 2003). Owing to its relatively recent industrialisation, democratisation and consequent dramatic changes in demography and society (Lee, 1999, 2004; Chang, 2004), the state of the Republic of Korea has recently turned its attention to some core social problems and democratically driven demands to which most Western industrialised states have had to develop responses for over a century.

Australia, in its short history as a sovereign nation, has had a much longer engagement with social policy than has Korea. There are both similarities and contradictions that emerge when one compares Australia with Korea and this poses challenges to finding suitable theoretical approaches to understanding the countries' comparative responses to demographic change and policy developments. There is strong appeal for policy makers to examine different ways of addressing core social problems such as those that emerge with each generation in post-industrial states; however, can these policy responses be easily reconciled given diverse cultural and historical contexts? In one sense the trajectories and initial political cultures for the two social policy regimes are almost contrary to one another. Australia, with its 'wage-earner welfare state' (Castles, 1985) model, emerging from an egalitarian political culture, its more recent responses to its marginalised Indigenous population and the current turn toward a neo-liberal governance model, is distinctive. It bears little similarity to

1 For simplicity's sake, throughout this book South Korea, or the Republic of Korea, will be referred to as Korea.

Korea's rapid transition from an agrarian to an industrial market under totalitarian regimes and subsequent democratisation, and a 'productivist' welfare response to social needs currently reflected in the modern Korean welfare state. However, given the widespread impact of globalisation on modern industrialised democratic states, the generally accepted 'crisis' of the traditional welfare state and the key generational problems both countries are experiencing, there are some similarities.

The chapters of this book focus on the search for new ideas on how to address core social policy issues such as: the social support needs of an ageing population; support for intergenerational care; young people and the Internet; public health care and population policies. These issues are of deep interest to policy-makers and government and community leaders in both countries. The ideas presented in this book are some of the ideas that will determine the nature and quality of the future in Australia and Korea.

As a more established welfare state, Australia offers tested ways of addressing social needs and problems. There has been a great deal of interest from Korea's government and non-government organisations (NGOs) in some of the models of delivery of social services in Australia, particularly in the fields of aged care, health and children (Phillips & Jang, 2005). This interest is partly based on a need to look beyond the United States and Europe for ideas about how to address the consequences of late industrialisation, but may also be due to a conception of the Australian model as an efficient and effective welfare state. However, in the past decade or so, many welfare state scholars in Australia consider recent changes and trends in the Australian situation to be bleak and regressive (Saunders, 2002; Mendes, 2003; Jamrozik, 2005; McClelland & Smyth, 2006). Therefore, in regard to social policy developments, in a broad sense, Australia and Korea are heading in opposite directions. The Korean government is seeking to build a more effective set of policies to improve the social protection of its citizens as a direct result of its ever-strengthening democracy, whilst the current Australian Government, which has been in power for nearly 10 years, has embarked on a program of dismantling or weakening its social protection functions as it pursues an ever more efficient, individualistic, market-driven model of 'enabling' welfare.

As an interdisciplinary set of writings the chapters have no single theoretical or political position as each author brings his or her own perspectives to their areas of expertise. Although the welfare state is not an explicitly *stated* interest in the following chapters of this book, it is hoped that this chapter will provide a framework for viewing the different countries' formal approaches to managing social problems. This chapter explores the distinct welfare state developments in Australia and Korea as a way of painting a political and social backdrop for the ensuing discussions by authors from both countries.

Defining the welfare state

The idea of the welfare state is complex, often contested and can be viewed or analysed from a range of perspectives. Jamrozik observes that social welfare "implies a set of provisions and mechanisms designed to ensure a certain standard of living for a country's population, especially delivering for those who, for whatever reason, are unable to provide such conditions by themselves and need assistance from society" (2005: 2). Jamrozik also draws attention to broader political understandings such as Jens Alber's (1985) idea of the welfare state as "a polity in which state responsibilities extend beyond the mere maintenance of internal order and external security to a public responsibility for the wellbeing of citizens" and that it can be viewed as indicative of an affluent society in which the state strives for economic growth as a solution to wellbeing, or indeed for intervention into the economy to ensure more equal distribution of the benefits of economic growth (as cited in Jamrozik, 2005: 3).

The redistributive role of the welfare state has also been highlighted in the context of globalisation due to an increasing need for the state to act as a buffer to protect its citizens from the negative effects of global capitalism and to ameliorate the effects of the globally integrated domestic free-market economy. It is also at this nexus that welfare states have been most affected and consequently restructured and redefined. This is clearly the case with the contemporary Australian welfare state and, in the Korean context, is the environment in which its welfare state model has been formulated.

Comparative welfare state studies have drawn heavily on the work of Esping-Anderson's (1990) influential typology outlined in his 'three regimes theory', which divides established welfare states into liberal, corporatist or social democratic models. However, due to the effects of globalisation, as well as 'the welfare state crisis' and the growth of welfare states in Asia, this is now viewed as a dated model. Esping-Anderson has acknowledged, in later work, that the three regimes theory is no longer sufficient to cover the changes to the welfare state in the late 20th and early 21st century world. The idea of a 'crisis of the welfare state' is pervasive and is linked to three key factors: trade-offs between egalitarianism and employment, the narrowing effect of globalisation on domestic social policy choice, and the global phenomenon of the ageing population (Esping-Anderson, 1996: 2). Many commentators (Esping-Anderson, 1996; Jamrozik, 2005; McMahon et al, 1996) believe that the crisis of the welfare state is linked to market failure – as many as those who attribute it to welfare state failure in terms of achieving overall social wellbeing. What is overwhelmingly agreed upon, is that the dominance of neo-liberalism and free market economics has meant that most welfare states are suffering under processes of deregulation, privatisation and residualism (or safety net welfare). As demonstrated in the current Australian context, neo-liberalism brings a strong ideological position that promotes anti-dependency and a highly individualist social view and it strives for minimal state intervention in the lives of families and individuals, preferring the family or civil society organisations to be the central providers of welfare or well-being. This shift has led Jamrozik to develop the notion of the 'post-welfare state' which, as a minimalist state, provides minimum income support rather than act in a redistributive way and to actively encourage inequality by basing social policy on a philosophy of competition (2005: 10–11). It also reflects a shift away from a citizenship rights-based model of welfare to one that delineates between the deserving and undeserving recipient of state support or social protection.

Crucial, and importantly linked to the social, political and economic conditions of the rapidly emergent Korean welfare state, are the links between democracy and redistribution. Jamrozik observes that, "social policy in the welfare state meant the application of democratic values and principles of equality and fairness to the decisions of governments on the allocation of resources through redistribution of the economic surplus generated in the economy" (2005: 11). This democratic process is about managing the economy, not necessarily intervening in market mechanisms, a view that is often a key economic argument against state expenditure or wealth redistribution. For Jamrozik, a properly functioning welfare state has both a 'facilitating' or enabling function and a 'maintaining' or controlling function so that it works to facilitate economic growth whilst protecting its citizens against the ill effects of disadvantage or inequality (2005: 12).

In his recent reflections on the future of the welfare state, Esping-Anderson observes that it is important for the welfare state to be viewed as a social investment, not an economic cost to the state (2002: 9). He also proposes that in considering a new welfare state model for the future, there are key social policy commitments that must underlie such a structure. These include the specific value of investing in families as a means of ensuring the productive contribution of children in the future, and gender equity policies that should not be regarded as simply 'a concession to women's claims' but as a means of addressing national fertility, childhood poverty and future labour shortages, crucial aspects of 'any positive post-industrial equilibrium' (Esping-Anderson, 2002: 10). He also raises concerns about the key generational issue of ageing and emphasises the need for "*intergenerational equity* (a fair distribution of the costs of future retirement between workers and retirees) and *intergenerational justice* (safeguarding the welfare of the weakest, both in working life and in retirement)" (2002: 24). However Esping-Anderson also warns against applying a single design to diverse welfare systems even though most face similar social problems (2002: 25). Although Esping-Anderson's and his colleagues' project of anticipating the needs of a new type of welfare state has a primarily European focus, it offers important reflections on the future of all welfare states and the remarkably similar pressures that all welfare states are facing.

The Australian welfare state

The historical origins of Australia's welfare state are related to the federation in 1901 of its separate colonies as states under a national government that became responsible for gathering income tax. Beginning with a means-tested national pension scheme that was funded out of general revenue in 1908, national social policy grew gradually, responding to major social and economic events and changes such as Australia's participation in World War Two. There was a peak in social policy development between 1941 and 1949, when basic legislative and service components were introduced. During this time poverty was recognised as a key problem and the government introduced core social security payments such as child endowment; funeral benefits for deceased pensioners; some maternity allowances; widow's pensions and unemployment, sickness and pharmaceutical benefits. The second peak of social policy development was in the 1970s, responding to strong women's and labour movements and a social democratic ideal of the welfare state. The Labor government of the time introduced radical initiatives such as universal health care, free tertiary education, Indigenous self-determination strategies, sole parents benefits and funding for women's policy and child care. Since then, there have been sweeping changes and consolidations based on which political party has been in power, but external factors associated with globalisation have driven a universal tendency toward an economic rationalist approach to social policy.

Many Australian social welfare researchers (Jamrozik, 2005; Mendes, 2003; Pusey, 2003; Saunders, 2002) are critical of the current directions of Australian social policy. There is broad agreement that there has been a dramatic increase in inequality and that the punitive nature of recent welfare reforms is creating an underclass of the most disadvantaged. Within what is described in Australia as a 'left wing' and 'right wing' political divide, however, there are some researchers who still identify with a right wing position, promoting the value of increased marketisation of welfare and advising on the direction of the current government's welfare reforms (Saunders & Tsumori, 2002).

Historically, Australia's welfare state is based on egalitarianism. This was due to its direct link to the establishment of a basic wage as a measure of social security benefits, and its focus on promoting full employment and a relatively low number of 'working poor' (Mendes, 2003: 27). Under the short but dramatic reign of the Whitlam Labor government (1973–75) and during the years of the Hawke and Keating Labor governments (1983–96), it had also maintained some key functions of a more redistributive or social democratic model. These were the nationally state funded old age, unemployment, disability and sole parent pensions/benefits, free public school education and a national state-provided health care system, Medicare. The Australian electorate has shown in successive general elections that it considers these social policy objectives as pillars of the Australian welfare state and characteristic of our 'fair go' society; and, as Michael Pusey's research found, many Australians did not want to 'end up like America' (2003: 182). A factor reflecting how we might end up like America, is evident in the increase in poverty due to the steady erosion of our protective wages system, our health system, our education system and our general recognition of the role of welfare. Under the Howard Coalition government the sense of egalitarianism appears to be giving way to a purer liberal welfare state model. There is a sense in the Australian community that the nation's closer economic, political and security ties to the USA are also bringing closer alignment in approaches to welfare provision, often viewed as a highly divided rich/poor social model.

Current welfare services expenditure[2] in Australia is 2.3 per cent of GDP or, based on 2003 data, $17.1 billion, which is average within the OECD countries. Of this total, $11.9 billion was funded by sources within the government sector and the remaining $5.2 billion by non-government sources (AIHW, 2005: 4). However, Australia's

---

2 Total social expenditure by Australian governments, non-government community service organisations and households in 2002–03 was estimated at $103.8 billion. Of this, $52.0 billion was social security benefits and other cash payments; $34.7 billion was mandatory employer-funded superannuation; the remaining $17.1 billion was spent on the provision of welfare services (AIHW, 2005: 1).

historically strong and effective welfare state has shifted toward what Gilbert terms an enabling state, where the government is working hard to create a social and political atmosphere of public support for private responsibility (2004: 43). In this model the governing principles of the enabling state, which relies on the private effort and responsibility of citizens and non-government organisations, are embedded in larger ideas that differentiate the 'enabling state' from the 'conventional welfare state' paradigm. Gilbert points out that this is measured by how far away it shifts from the 'ideal' social democratic welfare state "which has been widely considered the most generous and comprehensive arrangement for social protection" (2004: 43). The enabling state is characterised by market-oriented approaches to welfare, including privatisation of welfare services, and a belief that the market is more efficient and therefore better at everything. This is very much the ideology of the current Australian Government. It has pursued an agenda, through deregulation, privatisation, and industrial relations, taxation and welfare reform that has clearly shifted the onus of care and social support from the state to the individual.

A further characteristic of the current politics of the Australian Government has meant that, along with the impact of a 'reformist' economic agenda, social policy has also been dramatically affected by strong social conservative views. This had had the effect of turning back social policy progress in the areas of women's status, equality and security, race and cultural relations, protection and security for sole parents, security for gays and lesbians, and the imposition of national security at the expense of individual freedoms.

Australian welfare reform, 1999 to 2006

The best example of the effects of social conservatism and neo-liberalism is in the Australian Government's welfare reform agenda. The key principle of this agenda is the move from dependency to self-reliance; and this is played out in the theme of 'mutual obligation'.

Economic cost and the growth in the cost of welfare were key arguments for the government's reform agenda that's aim was to reduce the cost of welfare and reduce the number of people dependent on the state for income support. The Australian Government spent $23 billion on income support for working-aged people from 2001–2002 and $52 billion overall on social security benefits and old age pensions in 2003–04. Specific groups such as people on disabilities pensions, sole parents and long term unemployed were targeted by these reforms. Australia's high rate of family joblessness, 850,000 children live in 435,000 such families was also raised as key motivation for reform (Department of Family and Community Services, 2004). In 1999 the Australian Government embarked on its welfare reform agenda, beginning with a formal review of the state of Australian welfare.

In the process of the review, the concept of social obligation was used to develop the concept of 'mutual obligation'. The review report stated that these obligations are reciprocal and should extend across a whole community. It also stated that business, individuals and communities should have social obligations and should be incorporated into welfare reform. The idea of social partnerships emerged; as it was argued that the main reason for supporting a broad application of mutual obligation was because it would benefit welfare dependent people, by preventing entrenched social exclusion (Australian Government, 2000).

As broad concepts of mutual obligation evident in the review were translated into bureaucratic practices, they became rigid and punitive and, as Saunders (2002) observed, are now driven by the overriding need to reduce costs Social security policy had become obsessed with debates over means rather than ends. "These changes are part of a broader strategy to shift blame away from the failure of the government to address poverty effectively onto the limitations of those who rely on the system for income support" (Saunders, 2002: 57).

Mutual obligation, the idea that those who receive assistance in times of need should be required to 'give something back', is based on the idea that a strong framework of obligation will encourage people to move from welfare to work and is seen as the solution to idleness among the unemployed and a response to the unpopularity of a welfare system that is losing support from those who pay for it.

Although developed theoretically by Lawrence M. Mead (1986) in *Beyond Entitlement: the Social Obligations of Citizenship*, it was first applied by Prime Minister Tony Blair in the United Kingdom, where in his words, there was

a perceived political need to restore public trust and confidence in the welfare state.

In the context of this section of the chapter, mutual obligation is clearly an apt mechanism for the 'enabling state' and essentially relies on individual, not state, responsibility. Although it began with a focus on young people in 'work for the dole' programs, in each successive stage of reform the net for welfare recipients within the mutual obligation framework has been widening. Its impact has been highly punitive and people who are most disadvantaged are at greater risk of poverty than before. It works on a system whereby benefits are denied if obligations such as attending an interview or responding to a letter are not met. Now that the net includes sole parents, who are required to obtain work when their children reach school age and people with disabilities or chronic illness, who must seek and obtain part-time work, the notion of targeted welfare has also disappeared. Since 2006, this extended group of people who rely on the state for income support are now described as *failing* to meet obligations and are placed into a 'financial case management' system, a process contracted out to non-government agencies to make judgments about whether people who *fail* should get emergency support to help them survive periods without any income support due to *failing* to meet requirements. The risk of this system is that rather than pushing the most marginalised people into work, it may push them into dire poverty and loss of dignity as they are forced to depend on demeaning hand-outs in the form of credit for a specific supermarket chain.

The Australian Government's welfare reform program, in partnership with reduced intervention into the labour market to ensure employment, reflects the depth of change in the Australian welfare state in the past decade or so. There are many other examples, in current Australian social policy where there are equally cogent changes reflecting a shift away from a welfare state to an enabling state. Knowledge of Australia's recent and historical transformations is central to an understanding of the current Australian welfare state. In the context of this book about generational change in Australian and Korea, understanding the current nature and place of social protection or welfare in Australia is central to considering the types of policy responses that will have to be developed in the future to address the impact of changes across discrete generations.

The Korean welfare state

In the broader disciplines of comparative welfare state scholarship and policy studies, Korea is seen to have some unique and intriguing characteristics. It has been variously described as functioning under 'developmental liberalism' (Chang, 2004: 127), as a Confucian welfare state (Sung, 2003: 384; Holliday, 2000: 706), as a 'productive welfare state' (Kwon, 2002: 2), or operating in a 'development-universalist mode' within 'productivist welfare capitalism' (Gough, 2000: 14; Shin & Shaw, 2003: 335). The struggle in scholarship to categorise or describe the Korean welfare state reflects the Eurocentricity of welfare state theory and the relative newness of social policy in Northern and Southern East Asian states. Gough and Kim, in exploring the application of 'welfare mix' measurement, determined that Korea has a genuinely mixed welfare system, with, for example, three-fifths of health expenditure coming from 'the market' or private sector (2000: 6).

Holliday discusses developing a typology for Korea as a welfare state, in an exploration of 'productivist welfare capitalism', drawing on Esping-Anderson's (1990) above-mentioned pivotal work of 'three regimes theory' (2000: 706). What is useful about Esping-Anderson's framework in this discussion is that the framework regards all welfare states as having emerged developmentally in response to capitalism, each type of regime relying on different post-war political influences. Based on Esping-Anderson's two key principles as first, a capitalist order and second, a welfare state that extends social rights, East Asian states such as Korea can be viewed in a consistent framework that acknowledges their 'particularism' (Holliday, 2000). Asian states have developed the productivist model of the welfare state, which is subordinate to economic policy, links social rights to productivity and is premised on overriding growth objectives, thus creating a further model to add to Esping-Anderson's 'three regimes theory' and resulting in four 'worlds' of welfare capitalism (Holliday, 2000: 709). As will be seen by the discussion below, this does apply to how the Korean welfare state has emerged but it is questionable whether it will continue to be an accurate typology as the relative newness of the Korean welfare state implies a trajectory that will change and mature.

The key themes about the emergence and current nature of the Korean welfare state can be summarised as:

- Korea's short experience as a welfare state
- The emphasis on extraordinary economic development in Korea
- The initial emergence of social policies under authoritarian regimes
- Globalisation and the East Asian economic crisis
- The utilisation of Confucianism as a 'cultural' justification in determining policy
- The state as welfare regulator rather than provider
- Demographic and relationship changes in Korean families
- The ageing population, and
- Other social problems that emerge in a post-industrial state, such as the fertility crisis, child protection and poverty.

Korea's dramatic transformation from an agrarian to an industrial society in a very short period of time is the single most important structural factor in the development of the Korean welfare state. The most dramatic social consequence of this process was its effect on the family, diminishing the extended family structure (Shin & Shaw, 2003) and the economic capacity of families to have children at the same rate (Chang, 2004). This has led to the increasing dominance of the nuclear family model and a decline in the capacity of families to care for ageing members. It is also linked, according to Shin and Shaw, to an increase in family breakdown through divorce, the fertility rate crisis and to young people choosing to live single lives (2003: 332).

It is important to note that the foundations of the contemporary Korean welfare state were established by authoritarian regimes, beginning in the 1960s. However, the concept and ideals of a Korean welfare state were established earlier, as they were included in the constitution in 1948 (Lee, 1999: 25). During the 1950s and up until the mid-1960s, Korea suffered extensive absolute poverty, with 60–70 per cent of the population estimated to be living in poverty, and was a high level recipient of foreign aid (Lee, 1999: 26; Henderson et al, 2002: 2). The extreme poverty was largely due to the destruction of national infrastructure and economy during the Korean War (1950-53) and posed a very bleak future for its large agrarian population (Henderson et al, 2002: 2). As Minns observes, the extraordinarily rapid economic growth following the post-war period, from 1961 to 1987, was facilitated by the state's capacity to implement a strongly developmental policy whilst being "insulated from demands of social classes which may have diverted it from its objective of industrialisation" (2001: 1025). This view applies equally to the role of women in this period which was defined by a traditional Confucian structure assigning women three distinct roles in Korean society: "family reproduction; productive income generation and; voluntary community work" (Jung, 2004: 2).

From 1961 to 1987 Korea experienced three different authoritarian regimes under an 'authoritarian developmental state' model, all with a similarly minimal commitment to social policy which was viewed as a political instrument only (Lee, 1999: 26). This period saw dramatic economic growth at 9.8 per cent a year over 25 years, contributing to a rapid rise in the overall standard of living and the transformation from an agrarian to an industrial society (Lee, 1999: 26). The repressive and undemocratic nature of the state during this period meant that the social policies that were introduced were selective and minimal (Lee, 1999: 26). This process became pronounced under The Third Republic, having made a commitment to abolishing poverty and establishing a welfare state. Although it was successful in reducing absolute poverty, wages were kept very low and welfare reforms were mainly administrative or the introduction of benefits for select groups such as the military and government employees (Lee, 1999: 27). Lee observed that the establishment of pensions for these groups was a means of securing loyalty to a government that lacked legitimacy at the time (1999: 27).

It was during the last decade of this period that a democracy movement emerged as part of a formal labour movement and two key social policies were established: a revised Medical Insurance Act and the National Welfare Pension Act (1973), although these were not put into effect until 1977 and 1988 respectively (Lee, 1999: 28). The Medical Insurance Law was the first major social policy on health, although initially it only extended to large workplaces with over 500 employees and a system for low income and poor people covered by the then restrictive Public Assistance scheme, called Medicaid (Joo, 1999: 390; Jo & Choi, 2002: 8). It was not until 1989 that the Korean population as a whole received compulsory cover under the national scheme (Jo & Choi, 2002: 8).

The model of employer-based pension and health self-insurance remains as a core part of the Korean welfare state. Various reforms over the period extended health insurance to encompass more of the population (some 42 per cent were covered by 1985) (Lee, 1999: 28). Nevertheless, in vast contrast to the government-funded Australian national health insurance system, Koreans have always had to pay, and still do, almost half of their total medical costs directly, even those covered under the Medical Aid Programme (Shin, 2000: 87; Jo & Choi, 2002: 10).

Key to the development of a welfare state is the promotion of gender equity. Although women were granted the right to vote in the 1948 Constitution, it was not until the government established the Korean Women's Development Institute that the idea of 'women's policy' emerged in 1983 (Jung, 2004). This was a relatively ineffectual body until 1987 when it gained important political influence in policy and governance development in government (Jung, 2004). Although there was a strong women's movement in Korea from the 1970s onwards it was reluctant to engage with the authoritarian state, and therefore operated through churches, notable for the promotion of core feminist claims for education for women and for their active opposition to sex tourism (which had been openly encouraged by the government in the post-war period) (Jung, 2004). As Jung notes the other site for demands for greater equity for women was universities, with the first women's studies course being established in 1977 at the Ewha Women's University, where they earned a reputation for promoting women's issues as key social issues (Jung, 2004). It was, however, primarily due to international and national pressures in the late 1980s that women's policy evolved into important legislative and programmatic change. This included the Equal Opportunity Act (1987), the Basic Plan on Women's Development (1985) and the Mother and Child Health Act (1986) (Jung, 2004). Despite these reforms, the causes and consequences of gender inequity were not addressed and it was not until Korea adopted a genuine democratic system in the late 1990s, that women's policy began to be effective (Jung, 2004).

Also during this period the Korean government provided some support for community-based organisations to establish themselves as social welfare services, focussing on day care for children, support for the elderly, and some support for people with disabilities (Lee, 1999: 29). The real development of a social policy response to people with disabilities was assisted by Seoul's nomination for the 1988 Paralympics, which resulted in dramatically changed attitudes within government and wider Korean society (Yun & Nam, 1999: 484). From 1988 onwards, a number of key social policies were established to assist rehabilitation and care, employment programs and assistance for medical, educational and care expenses (Yun & Nam, 1999: 485). However, the social policy response to people with disabilities relied more on institutional rather than home support and was primarily available in urban centres (Yun & Nam, 1999: 489).

Despite growth in welfare spending between 1987 and 1997, Korea still performed poorly in its overall social services spending – even compared to other East Asian states such as Indonesia and Malaysia, both of which spend around 11 per cent of GDP on welfare (You & Lee, 2000: 21). However, as You and Lee (2000) point out government spending is only a small part of 'the social policy problem' in South Korea. They observe that the government's economic policy of 'growth first, distribution next' still resounds in its current approach. This is supported by Gough and Kim's analysis of Korea's welfare state, where they observed that little had changed in the mix of private sector, public sector, non-government sector and families' welfare in the decade up to 1997 (2000: 6).

According to Huck-Ju Kwon (2002) and others (Kwon, 2000, Lee, 2004; Shin, 2000; You & Lee, 2000), the East Asian economic crisis precipitated a unique response in Korea, as one of the countries hit hardest by the crisis. He explains that Korea not only undertook significant economic reforms, but embarked on 'vigorously implemented social policy initiatives' in response to the crisis (Kwon, 2002: 2). This view is also shared by Shin and Shaw, who observed, 'one of the unintended consequences of the process of liberalisation and globalisation in South Korea has been the expansion of its welfare state' (2003: 337). The Korean government recognised at this time that they had previously given a very low priority to social policy and with a steep rise in poverty arising from the economic crisis, basic welfare needs were stark (You & Lee, 2000, pp 20–21). Lee also observed that despite following the IMF's neo-liberal agenda that was tied to its significant funding throughout the crisis, Korea 'pursued an expansion and consolidation of social welfare programs' (2004: 29).

What is important in Kwon's (2002) observations of Korea's response to the economic crisis is that although it returned to economic stability far more quickly and completely than did its neighbours it continued with a strong social policy agenda. Kwon also observes that, like the Japanese and Taiwanese governments, the Korean government maintains a welfare system that is prepared to regulate but not finance welfare through the redistribution of wealth from the rich to the poor as it could with a strong progressive income tax system (2002: 6). Although expenditure in the area of social assistance under the National Basic Livelihood Security system increased dramatically after the post-crisis reforms of the Kim Dae Jung (KMD) government, by nearly three billion won between 1998 and 2000, reflecting greater access to assistance, as well increased need in that period (Lee, 2004, pp 293–294), welfare spending still did not reach a strongly redistributive level.

According to Kwon (2002) it is most appropriate to view the Korean welfare state in the North East Asian context, as distinct from the South East Asian region. The key similarity between the North East Asian states is their reliance on a social insurance system (mostly self-funded), with higher income earners gaining most benefit from redistribution (Kwon 2002: 5). Between all East Asian states Kwon notes an important political similarity where authoritarian governments dominate social policy-making 'using it an instrument for legitimation' and as an instrument for economic policy rather than treating it as a competing demand of governance (2002: 6). This view is also supported by Joo's analysis of the political purposes of governing elites in their development of key social policies such as medical insurance law and minimum wage law (1999: 388). Kwon describes the two key elements that paved the way for the growth of a social policy agenda at the time of the economic crisis as being the failure of the bureaucracy to manage the economic crisis, and the change of government (2002: 9).

East Asian states' success in their pre-economic–crisis development had been at the cost of developing and funding a welfare state. It is from these characteristics that the idea of a 'developmental welfare state' emerged (Kwon 2002: 6). Prior to the 1980s Korea fitted this profile, with social policy being determined from above rather than from grass roots or community advocacy organisations. However, as Korea moved towards democracy, through the late 1980s and 1990s, critical voices about the welfare system were free to evolve but little happened to improve social protection for poor, disabled, unemployed and older people (Kwon 2002: 7). These issues were not addressed until the end of the decade, when Korea was seen to have achieved 'true' democracy. A shift away from the 'developmental welfare state' to the 'productive welfare state' was introduced by the Kim Dae Jung government in 1999, reflecting the incorporation of social policy as an integral part of governance and as an 'institutional means of keeping democracy and the market stable' (Lee, 2004: 293).

As with the pension and health insurance systems, it was in the early period of democratic government (1988–1992) that all social security payments (except family allowances) were introduced (Shin, 2000: 86). Social security was extremely constrained, however, and reflected “a Korean welfare model which stressed the role of the family, the partnership between public and private sectors, the development of human capital, and the avoidance of dependency on the state” (Ministry of Health and Social Affairs, 1994 as cited in Shin, 2000: 87). In 1998 unemployment benefits coverage as an employment based contributory scheme (Shin, 2000: 94) were extended to cover workplaces with 10 or more employees, and later that year, to all workplaces. In 2000 the government introduced a modern social assistance program, the National Basic Livelihood Security system (NBLS), and expanded the four social insurance schemes and new women’s policy initiatives (such as maternity benefits) and significantly increased overall welfare expenditure (Lee, 2004: 293).

Social policy for an ageing population was not developed in this period. There was no adequate response to the dramatically changing cultural, family, social and occupational arrangements that had occurred in the previous 20 years or so. In that time Korea had seen the doubling of its aged population from 1.45 million in 1980 to 3 million in 2000 (Mi Oh & Warnes, 2001: 703). This is an astounding statistic when compared with other countries: for example it took 115 years for France’s aged population to double, the UK 70 years and Japan more than 30 years (Mi Oh & Warnes, 2001: 703). By 1998 there was a pressing need for ageing policy in Korea. Cultural and personal views of filial piety (the expectation that elderly parents would be cared for by the oldest son and his wife) were held by only 19.6 per cent of the population by 1996, due to the spread of education, changed material and occupational aspirations, increased workforce participation by women, and outside-of-family leisure (Mi Oh & Warnes, 2001: 706). Also, the new generation of older women did not want to repeat their experience of looking after their mothers-in-law, and along with older men, wanted independent lives (Jang, 2005).

The previously discussed economic crisis of the late 1990s resulted in a dramatic drop in private income transfers to parents, reflecting, in part, the shift to highly urbanised, less stable employment (Mi Oh & Warnes, 2001: 706). The need for mobility and rapid urbanisation was a further result of increasing ‘commodification’ of labour, resulting in a type of housing, either shanty towns or high rise apartment living, that was not conducive to extended family living (Mi Oh & Warnes, 2001: 706). The proportion of people over 65 who lived with their families dropped from 77 per cent in 1984 to 50 per cent in 1994, with an equally dramatic increase in the number of older people living alone (Mi Oh & Warnes, 2001: 707). Media reports in 1997 showed an alarming level of abuse of the frail aged by their children resulting in death or suicide, reflecting the overall incapacity of the new Korean society to care for its oldest and most frail members (Mi Oh & Warnes, 2001: 709). Although there was a dramatic increase in state spending on the aged between 1983 and 1996, in health, mental health, home care and residential care, this expenditure tended to benefit only the very poor and the very rich (Mi Oh & Warnes, 2001, pp 710–718).

It was also at this time that the issue of child abuse was finally addressed in legislation; with the introduction of the Child Abuse and Neglect Prevention Act. As indicated by Doe (2000), social policy on child abuse is a recent development. Although the rights of children were recognised in 1988, when the Declaration of Children's Rights was introduced, the incidence and acceptance of physical abuse against children remained very high. Prior to the 1998, legislation to 'protect' children did not provide any definition or criteria by which to identify child abuse, nor any specific reference to physical abuse as maltreatment (Hahn and Guterman, 2001: 176). As reported in Hahm and Guterman's (2001) survey of epidemiological studies and policy responses to child abuse in Korea, physical punishment of children was widely accepted amongst parents and professional groups such as teachers. Although the issue of child abuse was forced onto the government agenda by the South Korean Women's Movement (as was the case in Australia in the 1970s, particularly in relation to sexual abuse), as well as by scholars and medical and social work practitioners, actual responses to child abuse in the public domain remained largely unchanged. Prior to the 1998 legislation, a number of non-governmental organisations had established services for reporting abuse and endeavoured to conduct public education about child abuse in order to counter strong Confucian traditions of child ownership and discipline that dominated thinking in families (Hahm

& Guterman, 2001, pp 169–170). Although research across the wider population showed a high prevalence of physical abuse, reporting was extremely low. Up until the late 1990s, it would seem, child protection was virtually non-existent.

In summary, the Korean welfare state emerged in the period of authoritarian governments, between 1961 and 1978 and growing incrementally in response to increased democratisation in the decade between 1987 and 1997, and expanding dramatically in response to the economic crisis of 1997, particularly under the influence of the Kim Dae Jung government from 1997–2003. There has been a growth in overall social welfare expenditure from 5.29 per cent of GDP in 1996 to 9.18 per cent in 2001. It is predicted that in around 30 years time, Korea's social welfare expenditure will reach the average level of other OECD countries, around 20 per cent of GDP, mainly due to new welfare programs growing in response to changing demographic needs (Moon, 2000 as cited in Lee, 2004: 298).

You and Lee (2000) see globalisation as having forced the Korean government to increase its social expenditure but suggest that the existing social policy framework in Korea requires a significant overhaul if it hopes to deal with key social problems. They point out that despite increased spending, the costs of education and health care have increased even faster, and they cast doubt on the government's capacity to cope with growing unemployment (You & Lee, 2000: 26). In their view the most important issue for reform rests with taxation, and they call for a distributive, progressive system and propose that its role in social policies requires redefinition (You & Lee, 2000: 26). They also call for less intervention in the quasi-private education system, which they see as draining poorer peoples' resources and excluding parents and teachers from educational policy decisions (You & Lee, 2000: 26). In a recent study of social security payments in Korea, Choi and Choe (2007) found that poverty reduction strategies since the 1997 East Asian crisis had not resulted in significant reductions in poverty. They found that 31.8 per cent of people who received payments and who were living below the poverty line, remained below the poverty line after the payments (Choi & Choe, 2007: 187). They also found that even though there was improved efficiency in the distribution of social security transfers there was little improvement in the effectiveness of such small transfers. Korean's poverty support payments are one-seventh to one-tenth of Western welfare states (Choi & Choe, 2007: 189). Choi and Choe conclude that Korea needs both to redesign its income transfer system and develop diverse social assistance programs aimed at preventing future increases in the number of people living in poverty (2007: 189).

Policy comparisons

The following tables show comparative timelines for the introduction of some key social policies or welfare state instruments in Australia and Korea. Although not comprehensive, these tables reflect the very different social, economic and political histories of the two countries. Of obvious benefit to Australia was its early democratic base starting in the colony of New South Wales in 1843 (and other colonies soon to follow) and nationally in 1901. Korea's late democratisation (widely acknowledged as 1992 with the first popularly elected civilian president) has meant that many social movements, such as the women's movement in the 1970s and 1980s, have had no access to or influence on policy development until recently (Phillips & Jang, 2005).

More detailed examination of specific policy areas reveals further complexity and difference between the two countries' social and cultural contexts. For example, this chapter has barely mentioned Australia's Indigenous population, which is highly overrepresented in all welfare needs groups. Korea does not have this specific configuration as part of its demography nor in its demands for social protection.

Table 1.1.
Comparative table of key social policies Australia & South Korea

Social Policy	Australia	Date Intro	Govt Level	South Korea	Date Intro	Govt Level
Old age pension	1st means-tested old age pension	1908	National	1st pensions for civil servants	1960	National
	Universal old-age pension	1973-75		National Welfare Pensions Act	1994	National
	Means tested	1976		National Basic Livelihood & Social Insurance	2000	National
	74% of >65yr olds rely on govt pension for main income source	2005				
Unemployment Benefit	Intro of Commonwealth unemployment and sickness benefits - flat-rate payments from general revenue - means tested	1945	National	Expansion of unemployment insurance to include workplaces of 10 or more & later al workplaces – employment contributory scheme of limited time	1998	National
	'Mutual Obligation' Reforms	1999-2005	National			
Health Insurance	Medibank free universal state funded health & medical	1972	National	Medical Insurance Initially only covered large workplace w/ 500 employees & a system for low income & poor people - Public Assistance scheme, called Medicaid	1977	National
	Medicare, small tax contribution from all income-earners	1983	National			
	Free for low income & children	1997				
	Intro of private insurance tax incentives & minimisation of bulk-billing			Whole population compulsorily covered	1989	National
	Reintroduction of bulk-billing for children & poor	2004	National			

Table 1.2.
Comparative table of key social policies Australia & South Korea

Social Policy	Australia	Date Intro	Govt Level	South Korea	Date Intro	Govt Level
Gender equity	Women's vote	1902	National	Women's vote	1948	National
	Women's policy Instruments & gender equity – & intro of Equal Opportunity legislation	1973–75 & 83–96	National & states	Introduction of Women's Policy	1983 -97	National
		1996 – 2005	National & states	Master plan on Women's Policy	1995	National
	Dismantling of women's govt department	1996	National & some states	Introduction of Equal Opportunity Legislation	1997	National
	De-funding of large # of women's orgs.	2005	National	Ministry of Gender Equality established	2001	National
	Change of portfolio from Status of Women to Women's Issues		National	**Women's Policy Coordination Committee**	2002	National
Child protect-ion	Early legislation covering institutions & child welfare	1920s–1960s	States	Declaration of Children's rights	1988	National
	Beginning of deinstitutionalisation of children in state care	1970s	States	1st Child Abuse and Neglect Prevention Act	1998	National
	Legislation included provisions for all forms of abuse	Early 1980s	States			
Domestic violence & sexual assault	Refuges, sexual assault referral centres	1974 & early 1980s	National & states	Prevention of Sexual Violence Act	1994	
	Criminal legislation (AVOs etc)	Early 1980s	States	Prevention of Domestic Violence and Protection of Victims Act	1997	
	Family Law changes	1975 & 1995	National			

Conclusion

This overview of the nature and histories of key social policies in Korea and Australia demonstrates that there are many differences between the two countries, but it also shows that there are shared concerns about key social issues, as well as similar government responses to some of these concerns. In exploring the social and political nature of social policy development this chapter aimed to add to an understanding of the range of responses to challenges brought about by important demographic changes in Australia and Korea that are addressed in the following chapters.

This chapter has also presented some theoretical ideas about how to view the Australian and Korea welfare states, noting the rise of Asian welfare states as a key interest and challenge to a previously Eurocentric scholarship in the field. Drawing on the work of welfare state scholars in Australia and Korea, the above discussion also demonstrates the lively critical engagement of researchers of social policy in both countries. This chapter also highlights an interesting tension between the directions of the Korean and Australian welfare states: as Korea moves rapidly forward, embracing stronger equity and stronger participation by the state in social policy, Australia pulls away from culturally entrenched egalitarian approaches to welfare toward an 'enablement' model or more strongly emphasised market model. Some of the broader critical analyses reflected in the literature reviewed in this chapter are also articulated by the researchers in the proceeding chapters, providing some in-depth explorations of social problems arising for generational change in Australia and Korea. It is hoped that the forward-looking nature of much of the research reported in this book will contribute to governmental and societal responses required to address the specific needs of the rapidly transforming populations of the two countries.

References

Australian Bureau of Statistics, 1971. Special Article - History of Pensions and Other Benefits in Australia. *Year Book Australia, 1971* [online]. Available from: http://www.abs.gov.au/ausstats/abs@.nsf/Lookup/8E72C4526A94AAEDCA2569DE00296978 [accessed June 2005].

AIHW – *see* Australian Institute of Health and Welfare

Australian Institute of Health and Welfare, 2005. Health and Welfare Expenditure Series No. 24. *Welfare expenditure Australia 2002–03* [online]. Available from: http://www.aihw.gov.au/publications/index.cfm/title/10151 [accessed June 2005].

Australian Government, 2000. Participation Support for a More Equitable Society. *Report of the Reference Group on Welfare Reform*. Canberra: Commonwealth Government of Australia.

Bae K, 2005a. More Incentives Offered for Childbirth. *The Korea Times* [online], 18 March. Available from: http://times.hankooki.com/times.htm [accessed May 2005].

Bae K, 2005b. Concerns Grow over Pension. *The Korea Times* [online], 24 March. Available from: http://times.hankooki.com/times.htm [accessed May 2005].

Bidet E, 2002. Explaining the Third Sector in Korea. *Voluntas: International Journal of Voluntary and Nonprofit Organisations*, 13 (2), pp 131-147.

Bong-min Y, 2001. Health Insurance and the Growth of the Private Health sector in the Republic of Korea. *World Bank Institute Discussion Paper*. Washington: International Bank for Reconstruction and Development/World Bank.

Castles F, 1985. *The Working Class and Welfare*. Sydney: Allen and Unwin.

Chang K, 2004. Defamiliation in South Korea: The Demographic Dimension of Compressed Modernity. *International Review of Korean Studies*, 1 (1), pp 117–138.

Cho N, 2000. Policy Responses to Population Ageing and Population Decline in Korea. *Notes from Expert Group Meeting on Policy Responses to Population Ageing and Population Decline in Korea*, Department of Economic and Social Affairs, United Nations Secretariat, New York, 16–18 October 2000.

Choi, Jae-Sung and Choe, Jeong-Kyun, 2007. The Effectiveness of Poverty Reduction and Target Efficiency of Social Security Transfer in South Korea, 1999–2003. *International Journal of Social Welfare*, 16, pp 183–189.

Department of Family and Community Services, 2004. *Fact Sheets* [online]. Australian Government website available from: http://www.facs.gov.au/internet/facsinternet.nsf/research/researchfacs sheets.htm [accessed 20 June 2004].

Doe S S J, Cultural Factors in Child Maltreatment and Domestic Violence in Korea. *Children and Youth Services Review*, 21 (3–4), pp 231–236.

Esping-Anderson G, 1990. *The Three Worlds of Welfare Capitalism*. Cambridge: Polity Press.

Esping-Anderson G, 1996. *Welfare States in Transition, National Adaptations in Global Economies*. London: Sage Publications.

Gilbert N, 2004. *Transformation of the Welfare State, the Silent Surrender of Public Responsibility*. New York: Oxford University Press.

Gough I, 2000. Globalisation and Regional Welfare Regimes: the East Asian Case. Paper presented at *The Year 2000 International Research Conference on Social Security*, Helsinki, 25–27 September, Social Security and the Global Village, International Social Security Association Research Programme.

Gough I, and Kim J W, 2000. *Tracking the Welfare Mix in Korea*. Bath: University of Bath, UK.

Hahm H C and Guterman N B, 2001. The Emerging Problem of Physical Child Abuse in South Korea. *Child Maltreatment*, 6 (3), pp 169–179.

Henderson J, Hulme D, Phillips R, and Kim E M, 2002. Economic Governance and Poverty Reduction in South Korea. *Globalisation and Poverty Programs Discussion Paper* [online]. The Department for International Development, University of Manchester, UK. Available from: http://www.gapresearch.org/governance/KoreaReportAugust2002.pdf [accessed July 2005].

Holliday I, 2000. Productivist Welfare Capitalism: Social Policy in East Asia. *Political Studies*, 48, pp 706-723.

Jamrozik A, 2005. *Social Policy in the Post-Welfare State*. Frenchs Forest: Pearson Education Australia.

Jang H, 2005. *Early Ageing: The Life-Course Experience of Koreans in Australia and Korea*. PhD Thesis, University of Sydney.

Jo J and Choi K, 2002. Health Policy in Korea. *Discussion Paper*. Korea Institute for Health and Social Affairs.

Joo J, 1999. Explaining Social Policy Adoption in South Korea: the Cases of the Medical Insurance Law and the Minimum Wage Law. *Journal of Social Policy*, 28 (3), pp 387–412.

Jung K, 2005. Development of Women's Policy in South Korea. In Colebatch H, ed *Policy Work: International Survey*. New York: Lexington Press, 2005.

Kim C K, 2003 Women in the Korean Public Service. *International Journal of Public Administration*, 26, pp 61–78.

Kim I and Hwang C, 2002. Defining the Nonprofit Sector: South Korea. Working Papers of the John Hopkins Comparative Nonprofit Sector Project No. 41. Baltimore: The John Hopkins Centre for Civil Society.

Kim, Ki-tae, 2005. Neo-Liberalism, Wrong Recipe for Korean Economy. *The Korean Times* [online], 22 July. Available from: http://search.hankooki.com/times/times_view.php?terms=unemploym

ent+code%3A+kt&path=hankooki3%2Ftimes%2Flpage%2Fculture%2F200507%2Fkt2005072217550910980.htm&kw=unemployment [accessed July 2005].

Kim P S and Moon M J, 2003. NGOs as an Incubator of Participative Democracy in South Korea: Political, Voluntary and Policy Participation. *International Journal of Public Administration*, 26 (5), pp 549–567.

Kwon S, 2000. Economic Crisis and Social Policy Reform in Korea. *International Journal of Social Welfare*. 10, pp 97–106.

Kwon H, 2002. Advocacy Coalitions and the Politics of Welfare in Korea after the Economic Crisis. *Policy and Politics*, 31 (1), pp 69–83.

Lee H K, 1999. Globalisation and the Emerging Welfare State – the Experience of South Korea. *International Journal of Social Welfare*, 8, pp 23–37.

Lee H K, 2004. Welfare reforms in Post-Crisis Korea: Dilemmas and Choices. *Social Policy and Society*, 3 (3), pp 291–299.

McClelland A and Smyth P eds, 2006. *Social Policy in Australia Understanding for Action*. New York and Oxford: Oxford University Press.

McDonald P, 2000. Gender Equity, Social Institutions and the Future of Fertility. *Journal of Population Research*, 17 (1), pp 1–16.

McMahon A, Thomson J and Williams C eds, 1996. *Understanding the Australian Welfare State, Key Documents and Themes*. Croydon, Victoria: Tertiary Press.

Mendes P, 2003. *Australia's Welfare Wars*. Sydney: UNSW Press.

Minns J, 2001. Of miracles and models: the rise and decline of the developmental state in South Korea. *Third World Quarterly*, 22 (6), pp 1025–1043.

Mi Oh K and Warnes A M, 2001. Care Services for Frail Older People in South Korea. *Ageing and Society*, 21, pp 701–720.

MOHR (Korean Ministry of Health and Welfare), 2005. Departmental website. Available from: http://english.mohw.go.kr/index.jsp [accessed June 2005].

Park C, 1999. Economic Crisis and the Quality of Life in Korea. *Development and Society*, 28 (2), pp 229–257.

Park T K and Park S B, 2004. An Economic Study on Charitable Giving of Individuals in Korea: Some New Findings from 2002 Data. *Conference Paper*, 6th International ISTR (International Society for Third Sector Research) Conference, Toronto, July 2004.

Phillips R and Jang K, 2005. Strengthening the South Korean Welfare State Through Policy Transfer from Australia: The Experience of Social Work and Welfare Practitioners. *Research Report*, Sydney: Korean-Australian Research Centre, UNSW.

Prime Minister of Korea, 2004. Office of the Prime Social Welfare Minister. Available from: http://www.opm.go.kr/warp/webapp/content/view?meta_id=english&id=53 [accessed June 2005].

Pusey M, 2003. *The Experience of Middle Australia, The dark side of Economic Reform*. Cambridge: Cambridge University Press.

Rahn K, 2004. Child Abuse Soars Amid-Economic Slump *The Korea Times* [online], 24 August. Available from: http://times.hankooki.com/times.htm [accessed May 2005].

Saunders P, 2002. *The Means and End of Welfare, Coping with Economic and Social Change in Australia*. Cambridge: Cambridge University Press.

Saunders P and Tsumori K, 2002. Poverty in Australia: Beyond the Rhetoric. *Policy Monograph Number 57*. Sydney: Centre for Independent Studies.

Shin C S and Shaw I, 2003. Social Policy in South Korea: Cultural and Structural Factors in the Emergence of Welfare. *Social Policy and Administration*, 37 (4), pp 328–341.

Shin D M, 2000. Financial Crisis and Social Security: The Paradox of the Republic of Korea. *International Social Security Review*, 53 (3), pp 83–107.

Soh J, 2004. Child Abusers to Face Harsher Penalties. *The Korea Times* [online], 4 May. Available from: http://times.hankooki.com/times.htm [accessed June 2005].

Sung S, 2003. Women Reconciling Paid and Unpaid Work in a Confucian Welfare State: The Case of South Korea. *Social Policy and Administration*, 37 (4), pp 342–360.

Yun H K and Nam K J, 1999. Community Based Rehabilitation in South Korea. *Disability and Rehabilitation in South Korea*, 21 (10–11), pp 484–489.

You J and Lee J, 2000. Economic and Social Consequences of Globalisation: The Case of South Korea. *CEPA Working Paper No 17*. Korean Development Institute, Centre for Economic Policy Analysis, New School University, New York.

2

Australian demographic prospects, 2004-2050

Peter McDonald

Introduction

This chapter focuses on the potential demographic directions for Australia over the next 50 years. It also addresses key social and economic issues related to the transformations taking place in the make-up of Australia's population. These issues include the ageing of the population, future labour supply and the age structure of the labour force. As with most developed countries of the world, ageing is inevitable in the future direction of the Australian population but, as this chapter demonstrates, changes in demographic pathways may make a significant difference to the extent of future ageing. Given these trends, this should be a key national policy issue for Australia and should be central to economic, social and governmental strategies and considerations. However, despite the Australian Government's Treasury making reference to 'the three Ps' - 'participation, productivity and population' - as being key influences in Australia's economic future, it has tended, in its policy approaches, to emphasise participation and productivity rather than population (Department of Treasury, 2002).

There is a tendency for economists and planners to ignore the 'third P', population, because they work on the assumption that future demography is 'exogenous' to the economic models upon which planning is based. This effectively means that future demography will not be affected by future economic trends. Instead future demography is extrapolated from trends in past demography and then becomes the 'front end' of complex economic planning models. The implicit assumption of this approach is that the economy is expected to adjust to whatever future demography there turns out to be. Population policy in this context becomes an irrelevance. However, concern about the lack of a national ageing population policy was emphasised by an Australian Productivity Commission press release announcing its 2005 report 'Economic Implications of an Ageing Australia' which stated that, “in the absence of other policy actions to reduce fiscal pressure, taxation levels would need to rise by 21 per cent by 2044–45, or the debt burden of ageing would become twice as large as Australia’s GDP”. The Productivity Commission called for policy responses on a broad front and at all levels of government (2005b).

In contrast to the standard approach of economists, historical analysis of demographic trends shows plainly that demographic behaviour is strongly influenced by the contemporary economic and social situation. For example, in Australia in the early 1930s, the fertility rate fell to a very low level and international immigration was close to zero. A similar situation occurred in the mid-1970s. When the economy is unfavourable, births are delayed and immigration dwindles. When the economy is strong, birth rates rise and new migrants are attracted.

Rather than future estimates of demography being predetermined inevitably and inexorably by past trends in demography, they should be made in consort with envisaged future economic, social and environmental trends. If the Australian economy were to go into steady decline over the next 50 years, we could expect that population growth rates would be much lower than if the economy were to remain strong throughout that period. We cannot predict the timing of economic fluctuations (recessions and booms) but, at least, long-term demographic projections should be consistent with a clearly stated position about broad economic and social futures. Those who wish to assess the accuracy of demographic projections can then evaluate the reliability of this position. This is the basis of an argument for Australia to abandon the notion that its future demography is pre-determined and to evaluate, within the bounds of probability, what demographic futures are likely as an integral component of desired longer-term economic, social and environmental goals.

The future economic and social setting in Australia

The likely demographic future described in this chapter is based on the assumption that, in broad terms, the Australian economy will be strong across the coming decades. This is both the likely and the desirable future. This outcome is likely because sustained economic development of the two Asian giants, China and India, will underwrite continued economic growth of the Australian economy. The inevitable shift from oil-based energy to other energy forms will also be beneficial to Australia in the global context. Of course, Australia's continued economic strength is desirable because it will bring improved future living standards for Australians and increased wealth that can be applied to the improvement of environmental, economic and social infrastructure.

In summary the likely domestic implications of this future are:

- Substantial increases in standard of living. The Treasury's 2002 *Intergenerational Report* projected a doubling of the living standards of Australians between 2002 and 2040. This was confirmed by the 2005 Productivity Commission report: *Economic Implications of an Ageing Australia.*

- Major investment in new physical infrastructure. Infrastructure development has been neglected to a large extent in Australia since the 1970s. Massive new investment is required to address environmental degradation including greenhouse gas emissions, water supply, the transformation from an oil-based economy, and transportation and communications inefficiencies. Of course, this would need to be undertaken with a strong regard to short-term fiscal responsibility.

- A considerable demand for labour for the construction of new physical infrastructure, and new demands for service workers arising from increased living standards and the ageing of the population as ageing of Australia's population is inevitable, whatever reasonable assumptions are made about Australia's future demography.

- Substantial new investment in education and training infrastructure. This will be required to service the needs of the expanding economy and to deal with the rapidity of change in technology. We can comfortably predict that technology changes in the next 50 years will be faster than ever before in human history. The inevitable substantial changes in the way we live our lives, because of global warming, changes in energy forms, advances in water supply and sewerage, transport and communications, will demand highly skilled technological workers. Any country that is lacking in the highly sophisticated skills that will be needed to adapt new technologies to local environments runs the risk of failing to capture its share of global capital investment.

- Changes in social institutions to enhance social cohesion and the capacity for all Australians to share in the increased wealth of the country. Social disharmony is an obvious threat to economic progress. It can be addressed through changes in the structure of the tax-transfer system and through investment in social infrastructures such as health systems, early childhood education and care, community services and aged services. The capacity for workers to combine their work and caring responsibilities across their lifetime will be an important component of this outcome.

Labour supply: the essential integrating component

The essential link between demographic and economic futures is labour supply. The neo-classical economic model sees labour supply largely as an effective (elastic) response to labour demand. Potential workers will contribute more or less of their supply to the labour market depending upon the demand signals of the market, especially the level of wages. This model may have been relatively accurate in the past 30 years, but that was a time in which the potential labour supply grew rapidly because of immigration, the labour-force entry of the baby boom generation and the extension of the labour market to include much larger numbers of women. Between 1970 and 2003, the Australian labour force increased by around 85 per cent. On present population and participation trends, the future growth of labour supply will be considerably slower, between 10 and 20 per cent over the next 50 years (McDonald & Kippen, 2001; Productivity Commission, 2005a). Fundamentally, this turnaround in labour potential is the result of the high fertility baby-boom years being succeeded by 30 years of below replacement levels of fertility. Future labour supply is likely to be much less responsive to changes in labour demand than has been the case in the past 30 years.

With low unemployment and projected very slow growth of labour supply, particularly the supply of young technically-skilled workers, future labour supply is likely to be relatively inelastic to demand (giving rise to inflationary pressures) unless longer term planning of labour supply is in place. We cannot increase labour supply now by increasing the birth rate 25 years ago; we cannot increase the supply of workers with a particular skill now by increasing the training intake for that skill five years ago. While Australian immigration policy has been relatively responsive to immediate labour demand, the increasingly competitive international market for skills increases the unreliability of depending solely on short-term immigration policies to address labour shortages.

Without being explicit about precise numbers, a strong growth in labour demand will be an obvious effect of a strong Australian economy over the coming decades. Without a major increase in potential labour supply, Australia will not be able to undertake the massive physical infrastructure projects that it needs to improve the degraded environment, convert to non-oil based energy, improve water supplies and sewerage and eliminate transport and communications inefficiencies., Australia will also not be able to provide the number of service workers required by a wealthier and ageing population. Without an emphasis on young skilled workers, Australia will not be able to assimilate new technology as rapidly as needed.

The future of fertility in Australia

Future fertility trends depend upon more than past fertility trends. Five factors will be important for the future:

- Changes in the timing of births (the age of women when they have babies)
- Changes in young people's values, preferences and assessments of personal risks

- Changes in the characteristics of the population
- Institutional changes (work and family, gender roles)
- Economic trends and assessments by young people of economic risks

Timing

Over a period of about 30 years, first births have been delayed in Australia to ever-later ages. This has occurred mainly through a spread of the distribution of first births across a much wider range of ages than was the case at the end of the 1960s. A sizable proportion of first births still occur under age 25 (28 per cent of women aged 25 in 2001 had had a first birth) and so there remains scope for a continuation of the fall in fertility rates under age 25. This would tend to reduce the annual fertility rate as births are pushed out to some future year. On the other hand, there is recent evidence that women are having first births at a somewhat greater rate at all ages in their thirties. This means that a tendency to delay the first birth well into the thirties among more educated women may be reversing to some extent. This will tend to increase annual fertility as births are brought forward in time. Australian data on births by birth order are weak and this makes analysis of future trends very speculative. At best, current trends suggest that the falls in rates under age 25 will be at least balanced by the rises in the early 30s, producing a slight rise in annual fertility rates. Such a rise was already evident in 2005.

Values changes

As yet there is little evidence of a strong change in values amongst Australians towards having no children at all and the dominant value of a preference for two children remains (Weston & Qu, 2004). Data on young people's assessments of economic or personal risk are not readily available. However, the current long years of good economic times are a positive sign. Skilled labour shortages have also improved the economic outlook of the present generation of potential young parents. Finally, buoyed by the good times that have prevailed across their late teens and 20s, 'generation Y' are reputedly risk takers. Thus, from the perspective of values, we might expect Australian fertility to remain at least around its present level of 1.8 births per woman.

Changes in characteristics

In each successive generation, Australian women have become more highly educated and have been employed for a longer period before having their first child. This means that, when making a decision about having a baby, an individual woman's own human capital is much higher than it was for women in the past in Australia. Higher human capital means greater opportunity cost (lost income) from withdrawing from the labour force for a time. This is the logic that explains the fall in individual fertility as a woman's human capital level rises. A society-wide trend to higher human capital means that the aggregate level of fertility would also be expected to fall. This situation can be altered through strong government and private employer support, such as child care and generous parental leave provisions, for the combination of work and family. For example, in Nordic countries today where such work-family supports are very evident, the differences in fertility rates by education level of women have disappeared (Kravdal, 2001). Indeed, in these countries, the more highly educated women are beginning to have more children than their lesser-educated counterparts because their family income levels are higher. In Australia, however, the work-family balance remains problematic, and we could not expect the Nordic situation to arise in the near future. Also, Australian women are more likely than their Nordic counterparts, to want to work on a part-time basis, and the opportunities exist to do so. The new industrial relations arrangements could reduce the differences in fertility between Australian women because they are likely to have a greater effect upon women in jobs requiring a lower level of human capital than upon other women. All in all, these changes are likely to be a dampener on future Australian fertility.

There are other characteristics that potentially alter the course of fertility, such as ethnicity, religion and urban-rural residence. Overall, however, while these characteristics are associated with fertility, there seems to be a balance between their positive and negative effects on fertility. Thus, their impact can be largely ignored.

Institutional changes

In this discussion, institutional changes refer to the ways that society is organised that enhance or reduce the capacity of individuals to have children. The present Australian Government has demonstrated strong policy support of families by greatly increasing the level of government financial benefits received by those who have children (Howard, 2006). The new Maternity Payment is an outstanding example. There have also been gradual changes in the availability of child-care although child-care reform is the main type of institutional reform presently required in Australia in dealing with the work-family balance problem. Finally, workplace arrangements have shifted over the past 30 years in ways that are very favourable to the combination of work and family. Changes here include the ready-availability of part-time work in most jobs, flexible working hours, family leave, paid maternity leave (for about 40 per cent of the work force) and unpaid parental leave. The relatively high level of minimum wages has also played a role in enabling partnered women to work part-time but still earn sufficient income to meet the family needs. There is little question, however, that institutional changes have had a positive effect on Australian fertility in recent years. As mentioned above, the new industrial relations arrangements could reverse this favourable trend, but this is as yet unclear. There is also an argument that institutional changes have a greater effect because they change the psychology of childbearing; such changes provide to young people confidence that the social contribution of having children is valued.

The economic cycle

It is a lesson of history that a downturn in the economic cycle will reduce fertility rates. Until recently, economic cycles themselves have been taken for granted – what goes up must come down. However, in very recent years, some economists have questioned whether the amplitudes of these cycles will be as large as they have been in the past – on the grounds that we are now better able to manage the economy than we used to be. I am not so confident that a large crash is off the agenda, but I am confident that our capacity for avoiding it has increased. Accordingly, for long-term fertility projections, the best assumption that we can make is that economic circumstances will continue to improve. This is consistent with the projections of future living standards made in two significant recent government reports, the Treasury's *Intergenerational Report* (2002) and the Productivity Commission's *Economic Implications of an Ageing Australia* (2005a). Both of these reports estimate that living standards in Australia will be almost double their present levels in 40 years' time.

In summary, it is expected that fertility in Australia will not fall to the very low levels now prevailing in many European and East Asian countries. The more likely outcome is that in the future the fertility rate will remain around an average of about 1.8 births per woman. Note that this has been the average, with only minor fluctuations, for the past 30 years. Barring an immediate economic downturn, I expect a rise in Australian fertility in the short term.

The future of mortality in Australia

Mortality in the future will be related to our capacity to control causes of death through both curative and preventative measures. This in turn will be related to changes in aspects of lifestyle (smoking, alcohol consumption, diet, exercise, etc) and to advances in medicine. As death rates in Australia continue to be strongly related to economic circumstances, the future state of the economy and the distribution of its successes or failures will also play a role.

Over the past 30 years, life expectancy in Australia has been rising at the rates of around three years per decade for men and 2.5 years per decade for women. Similar trends have been observed in other advanced countries. There is hot debate among demographers as to whether this rate of improvement will continue into the future indefinitely or whether it will slow down. The argument that it will slow down is based on the notion that most of the potential for future falls in mortality is at the oldest ages, say, 80 years and over. A life saved at these ages adds much less life expectancy of life at birth than a life saved at age 60. Furthermore, it is argued that, as each cause of death is brought under increasing degrees of control, it becomes harder to make the next improvement because avoidance or cures for remaining diseases are more intractable. On the other hand, it has been argued that expectation of life has been improving at an approximately linear rate for some 200 years and there is little reason to expect that this trend cannot continue. The weight of opinion among Australian demographers is that the future is likely to look like the past: that is, the rate of improvement in life expectancy over the past three decades is likely to continue into the future (Booth & Tickle, 2004). This implies that official government projections ('the medium variant') greatly underestimate future expectation of life: life expectancy for women in 2050 is more likely to be 95 years than 88 years. The effect, about seven percentage points added to the proportion aged 65+ by 2099, will be felt largely beyond 2040.

Future migration levels

As argued above, so long as the Australian economy continues to be strong, the demand for labour is very likely to exceed its supply based on present levels of immigration. New demand for service workers including retail workers will be driven by increases in living standards and the ageing of the population. The building of new infrastructure will be very demanding of engineers and skilled trade workers. Similar workers will be required by the expanding mining industry. In a multiplicative way, the larger population will generate higher housing demand, resulting in higher demand for construction workers. All of these changes in turn will create demand for managers, accountants, computer programmers and so on. While Australia needs to focus on training Australian residents across all of these required skills, inevitably – as has been the case in Australia since the Second World War – high levels of immigration will be required to meet the demand. Canada, a country most similar to Australia in terms of migration policy and settlement patterns, has recently announced that it intends to increase its immigration intake to 300,000 per annum within five years (Beach et al, 2003).

The Australian Government reacted to these developments by increasing the size of its skilled migration program to its highest level ever in 2005-06 (98,000) and it has recently announced that the target will remain at that high level in 2006-07 (Department of Immigration 2006). The intake in the 'family' category was also increased in 2006 to 46,000. Thus, with the inclusion of the refugee and humanitarian intake, the total permanent migration program now numbers almost 160,000 per annum. On top of this, the number of temporary immigrants in Australia, most of whom have the right to work, has increased dramatically. Working holiday makers now number 104,000 per annum.

At the same time, young skilled Australians are being attracted to overseas countries at an increasing rate. Permanent departures from Australia have doubled from around 30,000 per annum a decade ago to 60,000 in 2005. The majority of immigrants are young Australians rather than former immigrants. Many are highly skilled. Most go to the United States and the United Kingdom. There is now a global labour market for skilled workers and the competition for them between countries and companies will become increasingly intense in the future. Nevertheless, Australia is heavily engaged in developing new approaches to the recruitment of skilled immigrants. As a result, it is expected that Australian will be able to recruit the immigrants it needs. Hence, for the reasons outlined above, it is anticipated that Australia's annual net immigration over the next 50 years will average out at about 50 per cent higher than its recent levels – that is, about 150,000 per annum. In a population projection, this could be implemented by increasing the level of annual net immigration by 2000 per annum every year for the next 50 years.

Three indicative projections of Australia's population

Based on the above discussion, three indicative projections of Australia's population are given below:

The Base Projection

In this projection, the Australian fertility rate is assumed to remain constant, on average, at 1.8 births per woman from 2005 to 2049. Life expectancy is projected to rise on a roughly linear basis throughout the period and reach 95.0 years for women in 2049. Finally, annual net immigration is assumed to remain flat at its present level of around 110,000. The age distribution of immigrants and emigrants is assumed to remain unchanged. Under these assumptions, the total population of Australia would increase from 20.1 million in 2004 to 29.6 million in 2049. The age distribution of the projected population is compared with the 2004 age distribution in Figure 2.1.

Figure 2.1. The Base Projection

Fertility remains constant at 1.8 births per woman
Expectation of life for women rises to 95.0 years by 2049
Annual net migration remains constant at 110,000

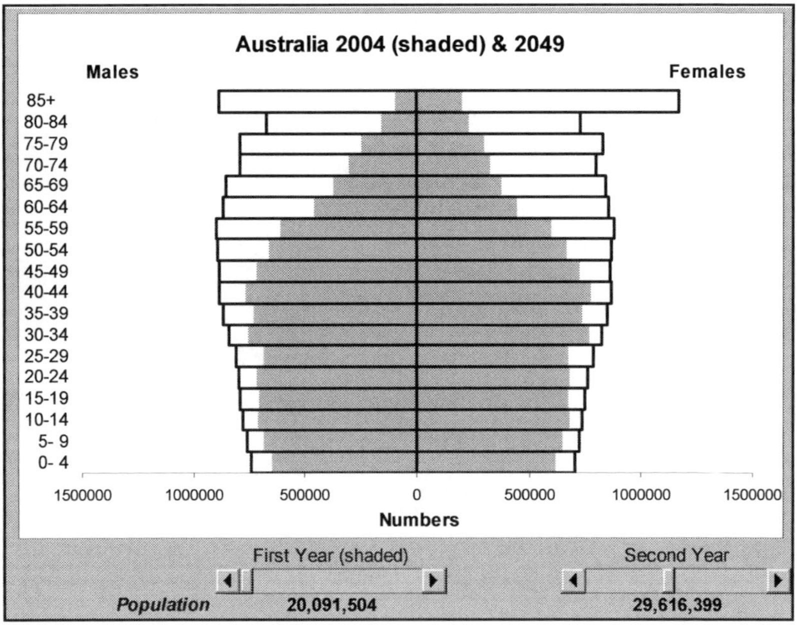

The Low Projection

In this projection, the Australian fertility rate is assumed to fall to 1.3 births per woman from 2005 to 2019 and to remain constant at 1.3 thereafter. This is a scenario that reflects the very low fertility rate now evident in many European and East Asian countries. Life expectancy is projected to rise on a roughly linear basis throughout the period and reach 95.0 years for women in 2049. Finally, annual net migration is assumed to remain flat at its present level of around 110,000. The age distribution of immigrants and emigrants is assumed to remain unchanged. Under these assumptions, the total population of Australia would increase from 20.1 million in 2004 to 23.9 million in 2049. The age distribution of the projected population is compared with the 2004 age distribution in Figure 2.2.

Figure 2.2. The Low Projection

Fertility falls to 1.3 births per woman by 2019
Expectation of life for women rises to 95.0 years by 2050
Annual net migration falls to 60,000 by 2019 and then remains constant

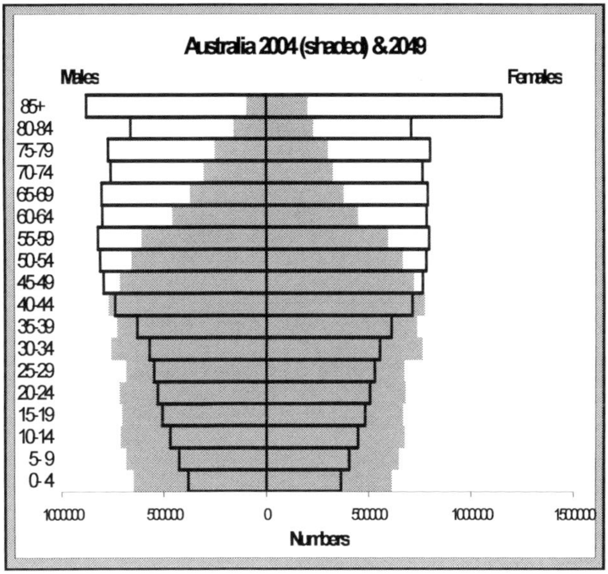

Figure 2.3. The High Projection

Fertility remains constant at 1.8 births per woman
Expectation of life for women rises to 95.0 years by 2050
Annual net migration rises from 110,000 in 2004 by 2000 per annum

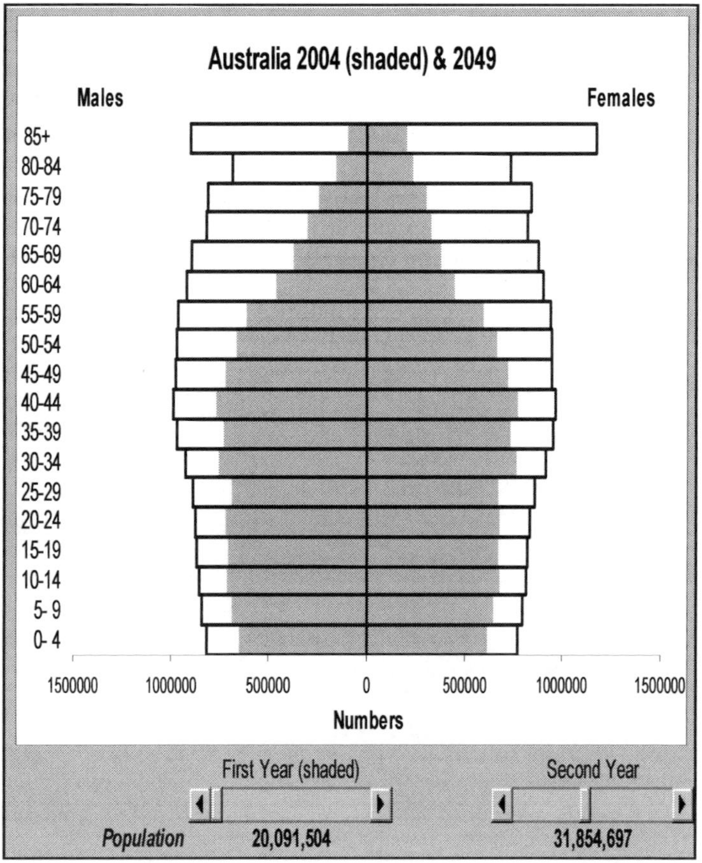

<u>The High Projection</u>

In this projection, the Australian fertility rate is assumed to remain constant, on average, at 1.8 births per woman from 2005 to 2049. Expectation of life is projected to rise on a roughly linear basis throughout the period and reach 95.0 years for women in 2049.

Finally, annual net migration is assumed, on average, to increase by 2000 per annum from an initial level of 110,000. The age distribution of immigrants and emigrants is assumed to remain unchanged. Under these assumptions, the total population of Australia would increase from 20.1 million in 2004 to 31.9 million in 2049. The age distribution of the projected population is compared with the 2004 age distribution in Figure 2.1 previous.

Under the Base Projection, the numbers in each age group in 2049 would be a little higher than they were in 2004 up to about age 50. Above age 50, the numbers in 2049 would increase gradually as age increases to become considerably larger at the oldest ages than they were in 2004. Under the Low Projection, the numbers in each age group by 2049 would be much lower than in 2004 at the young ages, but would become roughly the same as in 2004 by about age 50. Thereafter, the numbers at older ages follow the same path as the Base Projection with increasingly greater numbers at older ages as age increases. Finally, under the High Projection, the result would be rather similar to that of the Base Projection, except that the numbers at the younger ages (under age 50) would be somewhat larger at each age than was the case for the Base Projection.

Table 2.1, following, shows the results from the three projections for two important demographic indicators. The first shows a period of the increase in the numbers over 45 years in the important workforce ages, 25–39 years. These ages are important because they are the ages when the acquisition of the latest high technology skills is at their highest. In the Base Projection, the numbers increase by 14.7 per cent compared with 26.9 per cent for the High Projection. For comparative purposes, note that in the 45 years leading up to 2004, the numbers in this age group increased by 102 per cent. Thus, each of these two projections involves a massive fall in the labour force growth to which the Australian economy has become accustomed. It is for this reason, in combination with the arguments above about future demand for labour, that the High Projection is considered the most likely outcome for Australia. Comparing the Base and High Projections on the second indicator, 28.2 per cent of the population would be aged 65 years and over in 2049 while the percentage would be a little lower at 26.9 per cent for the High Projection.

Table 2.1. Two demographic indicators from the indicative projections

Projection	% increase in population aged 25–39, 2004 to 2049	% of population aged 65 and over in 2049
Base	14.7	28.2
Low	-20.5	32.2
High	26.9	26.9

In contrast to the Base and the High Projections, the results of the Low Projection are dismal: a 20.5 per cent fall in the number at ages 25–39, and 32.2 per cent of the population aged 65 years and over by 2049. These are the kinds of outcomes that many countries in Europe and East Asia are now actively trying to avoid. For Australia, such population outcomes would be associated with poor economic outcomes as people reduced their fertility in response to poor economic conditions and as the number of immigrants fell and the number of emigrants rose. The Low Projection is clearly an undesirable scenario for the future.

References

Beach C, Green A and Reitz J eds., 2003. Introduction. In *Canadian Immigration Policy for the 21st Century*. Kingston, Ontario: John Deutsch Institute, Queens' University.

Booth H and Tickle L, 2004. Beyond three score years and ten: prospects for longevity in Australia. *People and Place*, 12 (1), pp 15–27.

Department of Immigration 2006. Fact Sheet 20. Canberra: Commonwealth of Australia. http://www.immi.gov.au/media/fact-sheets/20planning.htm

Department of Treasury, 2002. *Budget Paper No 5: Intergenerational Report 2002–03*. Canberra: Commonwealth of Australia.

Howard J, 2006. Transcript of the Prime Minister The Honourable John Howard Address to the Menzies Research Centre, Theatrette, Parliament House, 18 April 2006. Available from: http://www.pm.gov.au/media/index.cfm?type=2 [accessed 20 April 2006].

Kravdal O, 2001. The High Fertility of College Educated Women in Norway: An Artefact of the Separate Modelling of Each Parity Transition. Demographic Research, 5 (Article 6), pp 187–216.

McDonald P and Kippen R, 2001. Labour Supply Prospects in 16 Developed Countries, 2000–2050. Population and Development Review, 27 (1), pp 132.

Productivity Commission, 2005a. *Economic Implications of an Ageing Australia*. Canberra: Productivity Commission.

Productivity Commission, 2005b. Long Term Ageing is Today's Policy Challenge. Media Release, 14 April 2005. Canberra: Productivity Commission. Available from: http://www.pc.gov.au/study/ageing/finalreport/mediarelease.html [Accessed 14 August 2007]

Productivity Commission, 1999. Policy Implications of the Ageing of Australia's Population Conference. Conference Proceedings,

Canberra: Productivity Commission. Available from: http://www.pc.gov.au/research/confproc/ageing/ index.html [accessed 14 August 2007].

Weston R and Qu L, 2004. Dashed hopes? Fertility aspirations and expectations compared. *Family Matters*, 69 (Spring/Summer), pp 10-17.

3.

Demographic changes in Korea during the period of 1960–2000

Ik Ki Kim

Introduction

The population of Korea was more or less stationary until the end of the 19th century. From the beginning of the 20th century, however, Korea has witnessed a series of population changes (Kim I K, 1987). The first sign of these changes was a decline in the mortality rate. Korea entered the first stage of mortality transition in the 1910s (Lee, 1980). The crude death rate (CDR) of 34 per thousand in the 1910s consistently declined until the period of the Korean War (1950–53). On the other hand, fertility did not show any significant pattern of change during the same period. The crude birth rate (CBR) was around 40 per thousand. The gap between fertility and mortality increased over time and resulted in rapid population growth.

The decade 1945–55 was, along with political, social and economic turmoil, a period of disturbance in Korea's demographic situation (Kwon et al, 1975). The liberation of Korea in 1945 from Japanese occupation coincided with the partition of Korea into North and South. The liberation and partition of the country brought about a vast redistribution of the Korean population all over the country. During the Korean War there was also of course a large number of casualties, particularly among young men; and there was a massive flow of refugees from North to South.

The population trends after the Korean War differ in many respects from those of earlier periods. Korea experienced a 'baby boom', which peaked in 1959. Since the beginning of the 1960s, however, South Korea experienced a major population transition, from a rapidly growing population to a moderately growing one, due to the consistent decline of the fertility rate. In effect, the South Korean demographic transition actually began at the beginning of the 1960s.

The rapid process of demographic transition in Korea was facilitated by the combination of rapid socio-economic development and the full-scale adoption of family planning programs (Kim I K, 1987). In Korea, mortality continued to decline after 1960, but the rate of decline was lower. The fertility level slowly declined after the peak year (1959) until 1965. Until this time, effective methods of fertility control were not widely practised. In 1962, the Korean Government launched a five-year economic plan and adopted a family planning program as a national policy initiating demographic transitions which began in Korea in the mid-1960s (Kim, 1987). Thus, this chapter will focus on demographic transition and, more specifically, it will address the general trends of demographic transition. These are: mortality transitions, fertility transitions and the process of population ageing.

General trends in demographic transition

Demographic transition is defined as changes in the fertility and mortality of a society as it makes the transition from an agrarian state to an industrialised and urbanised state (Coale, 1973). According to this definition, modernisation brings about demographic transitions; that is, a reduction in both fertility and mortality. Thus, from the perspective of modernisation, one of the most important features of this demographic transition is to be able to forecast the population trends of developing countries through the demographic model of developed countries.

As stated above, the rapid process of Korean demographic transition was facilitated by a national family planning program and rapid socio-economic development. The Korean Government implemented both the national family planning program and the first five-year economic development plan in 1962. The first five-year economic development plan was carried out successfully and since then, the Korean Government has continuously adopted five-year economic development plans.

Table 3.1 indicates the trends of GNP per capita and annual growth rates in Korea since 1960. GNP per capita in Korea was only US$79 in 1960. By 1965 it exceeded US$100. Since then, GNP per capita has continuously increased, exceeding US$1500 in 1980, increasing up to US$5000 in 1990, and reaching US$10,000 in 1995. But in 1997 Korea was hit by the Asian financial crisis; and in 1998, GNP per capita dropped sharply to US$6744. By 2002 Korea recovered from the crisis, and GNP per capita soared back up to US$10,013.

Table 3.1. Trends of GNP per capita and annual growth rates in Korea, 1960–2002

Year	GNP per capita (US Dollar)	Annual growth rate (%)
1960	79	-
1965	105	6.6
1970	253	28.2
1975	594	27.0
1980	1597	33.8
1985	2242	8.1
1990	5883	32.5
1995	10037	14.1
1998	6744	-6.6
2002	10013	9.7

Kim, Ik Ki. 2004. *Socioeconomic concentration in the capital region and its implications in the urbanization process of Korea.* A paper presented at a conference on 'Urbanization in Seoul and Ho Chi Min City: Lessons and Challenges' at Vietnam National University, June 14–16. 2004.

During the period of demographic transition Korea also experienced a rapid urbanisation process. This was linked to the Korean Government's economic policies throughout the 1960s, which were aimed at promoting export-oriented industrialisation through the support of labour-intensive manufacturing enterprises. During the first and second five-year economic development plans, extending from 1962 to 1971, the Korean economy grew at an annual rate of slightly less than 10 per cent. However, the growth of agriculture lagged compared to that of non-agricultural sectors. In this period, agriculture grew at an annual rate of 3.7 per cent compared to 17.9 per cent rate in the mining and manufacturing sectors (Ban, 1977).

Accordingly, the relative income level of peasants dropped. Luther (1979) indicates that a farm household earned about 71 per cent of an urban household's wage in 1962, but this figure declined to 61 per cent in 1970. This could be one of the many factors that brought about the massive influx of rural peasants into big cities, especially into Seoul. Rapid urbanisation concentrating on Seoul continued until the early 1990s. Since then, satellite cities surrounding Seoul, and industrial cities in the capital region, have grown much faster.

Urbanisation is a spatial manifestation of modernisation and is associated with various socio-physical phenomena (Choi & Chang, 2003). In Korea, urbanisation has been very closely related to industrialisation and economic growth. Since the 1960s, Seoul has been the centre of urbanisation in Korea. Internal migration was dominated by the centripetal movement of people from all over the country towards Seoul. In accordance with Seoul's dominance in the urbanisation process, Seoul has also been at the heart of Korea's economic growth.

Table 3.2 illustrates the population growth of cities as well as population trends in Korea from 1960 to 2000. The *total* population of Korea was 25 million in 1960, and it has consistently increased over time: to 31 million in 1970, 37 million in 1980, 43 million in 1990, and then to 46 million in 2000. The number of cities was only 27 in 1960, and this has also increased: to 32 in 1970, 40 in 1980, 73 in 1990, and 79 in 2000.

The *urban* population of Korea was only 7 million in 1960, with an urbanisation rate of 28 per cent. By 1975, it had increased to 16.8 million, with an urbanisation rate of 48.4 per cent. Korea has seen a continuous increase in its urban population and the rate of urbanisation. The urban population increased to 32.3 million in 1990, and then to 36.6 million in 2000. The urbanisation rate increased to 74.4 per cent in 1990, and then to 79.7 in 2000. As demonstrated in Table 3.2, the growth rate of the urban population has been unexpectedly high since 1960.

Table 3.2. Trends of population growth in Korea, 1960–2000

Year	Total population (1,000)	Number of cities	Urban population (1,000)	Urbanisation rate (%)	Growth rate of urban population (%)
1960	24,989	27	6,997	28	54.2
1966	29,160	32	9,780	33.5	57.4
1970	31,435	32	12,929	41.1	69.8
1975	34,679	35	16,770	48.4	52.0
1980	37,407	40	21,409	57.2	48.0
1985	40,420	50	26,418	65.4	42.0
1990	43,390	73	32,290	74.4	40.1
1995	44,554	73	34,992	78.5	16.1
2000	45,985	79	36,642	79.7	9.2

Source: KNSO, Population and Housing Census, www. http://www.nso.go.kr/.

The urban population as well as the total population have continuously increased, but between 1966 and 1970 the rural population's growth rate declined resulting in an absolute decrease in the size of the rural population for the first time in the recent history (Kim, 1987).

Table 3.3 shows the factors influencing the growth of the urban population from 1960 to 2000. Net migration from rural areas, the enlargement of urban areas, and the construction of new cities are factors that affected growth in the urban population. During the period 1960–1966, the urban population increased by 2.7 million. This was comprised of: a natural increase (42.1 per cent), net migration (40.5 per cent), urban area growth (9.3 per cent) and the construction of new cities (8.0 per cent).

In contrast to other periods, the share of net migration, almost entirely from rural areas, influencing urban population growth in 1966-1970 was exceptionally high, at 73.2 per cent. This is significant as 1966 to 1970 was the period of the second five-year economic development plan. Such a heavy shift of rural dwellers, especially of working age people also resulted in a higher dependency ratio in urban areas (Moon, 1978).

Another notable fact in the process of urbanisation has been the construction, since 1975, of new satellite cities around the established metropolis. This became especially significant in 1985–1990, when the Korean Government, concerned with the rapid growth of the urban population, especially in Seoul, began an intense period of constructing satellite cities to help redistribute that population.

As mentioned earlier, demographic transition in Korea was affected by both a national family-planning program and socio-economic development. Table 3.4 illustrates the demographic transition and related factors in Korea.

Table 3.3. Factors of urban population growth, 1960–2000 (Unit: 1000 persons, %)

Period	Urban population growth (in 1000s)	Factors of urban population growth (%)			
		Natural growth	Net migration	Enlargement of urban districts	Changing to city status
1960–1966	2709	42.1	40.6	9.3	8.0
1966–1970	3223	26.8	73.2	0.0	0.0
1970–1975	3842	47.2	45.1	2.5	5.2
1975–1980	4638	45.7	39.7	4.1	10.5
1980–1985	5506	44.4	36.8	1.3	17.4
1985–1990	5866	36.3	27.0	6.2	30.4
1990–1995	2727	72.8	7.0	1.3	19.0
1995–2000	1719	62.2	12.9	0.0	24.9

Source: Choi et al (1993: 11); KNSO. Population and Housing Census Report, each year.

Korean society experienced a major demographic transition from the early 1960s. During the period 1960–1985, both the fertility rate and mortality rate continued to decline, and thus the population growth rate continuously decreased. This demographic transition was affected by several intermingled socio-economic factors such as modernisation, economic development, urbanisation, and the national family planning program. Since 1985, the fertility rate in Korea has dropped to below replacement level and the mortality rate has remained stable with a slight decline. According to the Korea National Statistical Office (KNSO) projections, the population will increase from 47 million in 2000 to 50.7 million in 2020 and then begin to decrease (KNSO, 2001). This process of demographic transition may be due to factors such as sustained economic growth, the expansion of education, changes in lifestyle, and the full-scale adoption of medical insurance.

Table 3.4. Demographic transition and related factors in Korea

Stage	Period	Population growth	Fertility	Mortality	Political and socioeconomic factors
The pre-transition stage	1945–60	Rapid increase except for the period 1949–1955	High	Medium but high mortality during 1949–1955	Liberation, partition of the country, the Korean War, social turmoil, economic hardship
The transition stage	1960–85	Continuous decline in growth rate	Rapid and continuous decline	Continued decline	Modernisation, economic development, urbanisation, family planning program
The post-transition stage	1985 to present	Stable stage with negative growth potential	Under replacement level	Stable stage with slight decline	Sustained economic gro wth, expansion of education, changes in lifestyle, medical insurance

Source: Kim D S, 2003. Growth and transition in the population of Korea. Korea National Statistical Office (KNSO).

Mortality transition

Korea entered the first stage of mortality transition in the 1910s. The factors responsible for the decline in mortality were the prevention of infectious and contagious diseases and the improvement of environmental conditions and public health facilities (Lee, 1980).

Additional factors were the establishment of medical schools and medical facilities. However, industrialisation and urbanisation directly related to Japanese colonisation between 1910 and 1945 had little impact on mortality rates (Kim I K, 1987).

The Korean War (1950–53) had a great impact on the Korean population. War casualties were estimated to be 1.6 million, and the crude death rate rose sharply during this period (Lee, 1980). The crude death rate during the five-year period up to 1955 hit a record high of 33 per thousand and in 1955, Korea entered the second stage of mortality transition.

The primary factor responsible for the sharp decline in mortality immediately after the Korean War was the introduction of various new medicines. Improvement of sanitary conditions during the process of restoration from the war devastation also made a remarkable contribution to the decline in mortality. In fact, the rapid reduction in mortality took place in the absence of any substantial socio-economic development within the country.

After 1960, the pattern of a decline in mortality continued, but the rate of decline decreased. Improvements from this time onwards have been most attributable to rapid socio-economic development. This includes the expansion of health and medical, in both the public and private sectors, and a decline in fertility due to an increased adoption of the family planning program and the postponement of marriage.

Table 3.5 shows mortality trends in Korea from 1960 to 2000. The crude death rate in 1960 was 16 per thousand. Since then, the crude death rate has consistently decreased: to a rate of 8 per thousand in 1971, 6 per thousand in 1985, and 5.2 per thousand in 2000.

In an inverse proportion to the continuous decline of the crude death rate, life expectancy at birth has substantially increased over time. Table 3.5 also shows the trends of average life expectancy at birth since 1960. Life expectancy at birth in 1960 was 51.1 years for males and 57.3 years for females. Life expectancy has consistently increased both for males and females. For males, it increased to 62.3 years in 1980, 67.7 years in 1990, then to 72.8 years in 2000. For females, it increased at the same speed from 57.3 years in 1960, to 70.5 years in

1980, 75.9 years in 1990, then to 80.0 years in 2000. The continuous increase in life expectancy has brought about a corresponding increase in the proportion of the elderly; that is, the population is ageing.

Table 3.5. Trends in mortality and life expectancy in Korea, 1960–2000

Kim I K, 1992. A Comparative Study of Demographic Transition between Korea and Japan.

Table 3.6 shows the age-specific death rates (ASDR) by gender in Korea during the period 1970–2000. Since 1970, all of the ASDRs for both genders have declined greatly. The death rate for those in their 20s declined faster than the rate for those aged 30 years or above. In terms of gender, the decline was faster for females than for males. However, the difference between males and females becomes smaller as age advances. The extent of crude death rate reduction was smaller among women than among men, even though ASDR declined more rapidly for women than for men. This is due to the rapid ageing of the female population given the low level of mortality. In addition, the mortality patterns are different according to gender: the mortality for middle-aged adults is much higher for men than for women (Kim,

Year	CDR	Life expectancy at birth	
		Male	Female
1960(1)	16	51.1	57.3
1965	15(1)	52.7	57.7
1971	8.0	59.0	66.1
1975	7.7	60.2	67.9
1980	7.3	62.3	70.5
1985	6.0	64.3	72.8
1990	5.8	67.7	75.9
1995	5.4	69.6	77.4
2000	5.2	72.8	80.0

T.H., 2003). However, the gender differentials of mortality become narrow and the mortality pattern of men approaches that of women.

Causes of death are dependent upon a society's socio-economic situation. Causes of death in Korea have consequently differed from time to time in accordance with its socio-economic development. Table 3.7 shows the 10 leading causes of death between 1966 and 2000. Leading causes of death in 1966 were pneumonia and tuberculosis. Of the 10 major causes of death, six are diseases of the respiratory and digestive systems and infectious diseases. Between 1980 and 1981, however, the five most significant causes of death were three types of circulatory system disease, neoplasms and accidents. From 1990, the four main causes of death were malignant neoplasms, brain vein diseases, heart diseases, and traffic accidents. Such changes in the pattern of causes of death indicate that the sharp decline in mortality levels since 1966 has been due mainly to a reduction in diseases of the respiratory systems and infectious diseases such as pneumonia and tuberculosis.

Table 3.6. Age-Specific Death Rates by Sex, 1970–2000 (Unit: per 1000 persons)

	Male			Female		
	1970	1990	2000	1970	1990	2000
Total	9.2	6.6	5.8	6.8	5.0	4.7
0~4	4.7	3.7	1.3	4.5	3.2	1.2
5~9	2.6	0.7	0.3	2.3	0.5	0.2
10~14	2.1	0.6	0.2	1.7	0.4	0.2
15~19	3.5	1.2	0.6	2.5	0.5	0.3
20~24	4.2	1.5	0.9	3.5	0.7	0.4
25~29	3.8	1.9	1.1	3.7	0.8	0.5
30~34	4.0	2.5	1.4	3.3	1.0	0.7
35~39	5.5	3.7	2.2	4.1	1.4	0.9
40~44	9.1	5.4	3.6	5.3	2.0	1.3
45~49	14.9	9.0	5.5	7.0	3.4	1.8
50~54	22.4	12.3	7.9	10.0	4.7	2.7
55~59	33.1	17.1	12.7	14.2	6.9	4.5
60~64	47.5	26.7	18.2	20.4	11.1	7.0
65~69	72.9	40.8	26.3	31.9	18.5	12.0
70~74	95.5	64.4	43.7	49.1	33.0	23.8
75~79	225.21	97.0	74.6	179.21	55.9	44.0
80+	–	187.0	152.1	–	137.1	121.2
IMR2	40.8	14.3	6.1	39.9	13.0	5.9

Source: Kim T H, 2003.

Table 3.7. Ten leading causes of death in Korea, 1966-2000

Rank	1966[1]	1980–1981[2]	1990[3]	2000[3]
1	Pneumonia	Malignant neoplasms	Malignant neoplasms	Malignant neoplasms
2	Tuberculosis	Hypertensive diseases	Brain vein diseases	Brain vein diseases
3	Vascular lesions affecting the central nerve system	Cerebrovascular diseases	Heart diseases	Heart diseases
4	Malignant neoplasms	Accidents	Traffic accidents	Traffic accidents
5	Gastritis, duodenitis, enteristis and colitis	Heart diseases	Hypertensive diseases	Chronic liver diseases and cirrhosis
6	Accidents	Tuberculosis	Chronic liver diseases and cirrhosis	Diabetes
7	Influenza	Chronic liver diseases and cirrhosis	Diabetes	Chronic bronchus diseases
8	Heart diseases	Bronchitis, emphysema and asthma	Respiratory system tuberculosis	Suicides
9	Measles	Pneumonia	Chronic bronchus diseases	Hypertensive diseases
10	Bronchitis	Suicide	Suicide	Pneumonia

Notes: 1 Based on the abbreviated list of 50 causes of death in the 7th Revision of the ICD.
2 Based on the list of 55 causes of death in the 9th Revision of the ICD.
3 Based on the list of 56 causes of death in the 1995 KSCD (KNSO, Social Indicators in Korea, 2001: 270–272).
4 Deaths per 100 thousand persons aged 5 years or over.

Source: Kim T H, 2003.

Fertility transition

Table 3.8 shows fertility trends in Korea between 1960 and 2000. The crude birth rate (CBR) in 1960 was as high as 45 per thousand. Since then, the rate has continuously declined. While the crude birth rate declined only by three per thousand from 1960 to 1965, it declined sharply from 42 per thousand to 31.2 between 1965 and 1970. The reduction in the crude birth rate by 11 per thousand for this five-year period is a record high. Since then, the fertility level has steadily declined without interruption: the crude birth rate declined to 22.7 per thousand in 1980, to 15.4 in 1990, then to 13.4 in 2000. As with the CBR, the total fertility rate (TFR) has also sharply declined over time. The total fertility level in 1960 was as high as six, but declined to 2.83 in 1980. Since 1985, the fertility level of the Korean population has gone below the replacement level and has shown a consistent pattern of decline over time: the TFR decreased to 1.67 in 1985, to 1.57 in 1990, and then finally dropped to 1.47 in 2000.

Table 3.8. Fertility Trends in Korea, 1960–2000

Year	CBR	TFR
1960(1)	45.0	6.0
1965(1)	42.0	4.9
1970	31.2	4.53
1975	24.8	3.47
1980	22.7	2.83
1985	16.2	1.67
1990	15.4	1.57
1995	16.0	1.65
2000	13.4	1.47

Source : (1) Kim I K, 1992. p 57.
(2) Korea National Statistical Office, 2002.

Table 3.9 shows more specifically the changing patterns of age-specific fertility rates (ASFR) in Korea during the period 1960–2000. This table enumerates several important points. First of all, it indicates that most births were concentrated in the 35–39 age group, without exception throughout the whole period. Second, the majority of births were concentrated in the age group of 20–39 years during the 1955–1980 period. Third, ASFRs have consistently decreased for all the age groups between 1960 and 2000. Fourth, births for 15–19 year-olds and 40–44 year-olds have drastically declined since 1980. Fifth, there have been no births in the 45–49 age group since 1980. Putting all these findings together, we may conclude that the sharp decline in the total fertility rate is related to the shortening of the age span that women are inclined to give birth.

Table 3.9. Total fertility rates and age-specific fertility rates in Korea, 1960–2000

(Unit: births per woman, births per 1000 persons)

Age year	Total fertility rate (TFR)	Age-specific fertility rate (ASFR)						
		15–19	20–24	25–29	30–34	35–39	40–44	45–49
1955–1960	6.30	38	308	335	270	194	96	18
1960–1965	5.99	20	255	351	274	189	92	17
1965–1970	4.64	12	180	309	223	134	59	10
1970–1975	3.96	10	146	301	220	88	19	7
1975–1980	3.00	13	152	253	122	38	17	5
1980–1985	2.38	11	160	216	72	15	2	0
1985–1990	1.62	4	103	168	39	6	3	0
1990–1995	1.64	4	74	177	58	12	2	0
1995–2000	1.55	3	56	159	72	15	5	0

Note: The five-year TFRs and ASFRs from 1970–2000 are estimated through calculation of the five-year moving averages of the KNSO data for the period concerned. Source: Jun K H, 2003.

Reduction in fertility during the period of fertility transition in Korea may be attributable to a number of factors. Assuming that fertility is confined to marriage, the overall fertility level is generally affected by both the proportion of married women in the population and the extent of 'marital fertility' control. Control of marital fertility is achieved through contraception and induced abortion. In Korea, national family planning programs have had a tremendous impact on the decline in the fertility level since they were introduced in 1962.

As a result of these national family planning programs, the TFRs began to drop from 6 births per woman in 1960–1965 to 4.6 births per woman in 1965–1970. In 1966, fertility dropped more sharply in Seoul and other metropolitan cities because Korean couples wanted to avoid giving birth to girls in the Year of the White Horse (Kwon, 1977). Based on patriarchal and Confucian beliefs Koreans have traditionally thought that the Year of the White Horse is inauspicious for "the destiny of girls" as it implies "undesirable traits for women as wives" (Lee and Paik, 2006). Furthermore, induced abortions became prevalent in urban areas, and contraceptives began to be readily available from the early 1960s.

The rate of fertility decline was more rapid in rural than in urban areas because, beginning in the late 1960s, the Korean Government invested more resources in family planning in rural areas than in urban ones. In the early 1970s, the rate of fertility decline slowed to around four births per woman, but it later gained momentum by dropping sharply to three births per woman in the late 1970s, indicating the end of the first fertility transition (Jun, 2003).

The later phase of the first fertility transition began in the early 1970s when Korean couples internalised the concepts of desired family size (DFS), fertility regulation, and the value of children (Jun, 2003). This late phase has implications entirely different from those of the early phase of the fertility transition. Before 1975, traditional family norms had exerted strong constraints on Korean couples. Until then, most Korean couples did not internalise the idea that they would be able to achieve their desired family size through contraception and induced abortion. In cases of extreme poverty, unemployment, and difficulty in supporting a large family, Koreans were forced to participate in government-sponsored family planning programs, due to the increasing number of surviving children resulting from improved infant mortality (Jun, 2003). However, young men and women who married after 1965 played an important role in leading the fertility transition. They began to participate in voluntary fertility regulation at the end of their childbearing years from 1975.

Table 3.10 indicates the various factors affecting changes in the total fertility rates from 1960 to 2000. Up to 1990, the decline in the marital fertility rate made a greater contribution to the decline in TFR than the effects of marital composition. Also during this period, the role of contraception was very significant in reducing the marital fertility rate, especially between 1965 and 1990. Induced abortion was another important factor in reducing the marital fertility rate, but only up until 1975. The decline in the marital fertility rate due to the adoption of family planning programs did not play a significant role in reducing TFR after 1990. Since 1990, postponement of marriage made a rather greater contribution to the decline in TFR.

Table 3.10. Components of the percentage change in total fertility rates, 1960–2000

Year components	1960–1965	1965–1970	1970–1975	1975–1980	1980–1985	1985–1990	1990–1995	1995–2000
TFR changes (%)	-16.8	-17.6	-13.4	-24.6	-25.7	-18.3	1.2	-5.4
(a) Marital	-6.3	-3.7	-3.5	-5.6	-6.4	-6.5	-5.8	-9.9
Proportion Married	-7.6	-3.4	-3.7	-4.9	-6.7	-7.9	-5.6	-9.6
Divorce & Widowhood	1.3	0.5	0.2	0.7	0.3	1.4	-0.2	-0.3
(b) Age-specific	-10.5	-14.1	-9.9	-19.1	-19.3	-11.8	7.0	4.5
Contraception	-5.4	-9.5	-5.9	-23	-23.9	-13.4	-5.3	-7.4
Induced abortion	-5.1	-4.6	-4.0	3.9	4.6	1.6	12.3	11.9

Source: Jun, 2003.

As mentioned earlier, postponement of marriage has affected the reduction in the total fertility rate, especially since 1990. Table 3.11 shows the trends in age at the time of marriage from 1970 to 2000. The average ages at marriage for both males and females have continuously increased over time. For males, it increased from 26.7 years in 1970, to 27.8 years in 1990, then to 29.3 years in 2000. For females, it increased from 22.6 years in 1970, to 24.8 years in 1990, then to 26.5 years in 2000.

Table 3.11. Trends of average age at marriage in Korea, 1970–2000

Year	Age at marriage (M)	Age at marriage (F)

1970	26.7	22.6
1975	26.8	22.8
1980	26.4	23.2
1985	27.0	24.1
1990	27.8	24.8
1995	28.4	25.5
2000	29.3	26.5

Source: KNSO. Korea Statistical Yearbook. 2002.

Not only the postponement of marriage but also the increasing proportion of those who are not married has affected the decline in the total fertility rate. Table 3.12 illustrates the trends in the proportion of those who are not married during the period 1970–2000. The proportion of those who are not married for females aged 25–29 years increased from 10 per cent in 1970, to 22 per cent in 1990, then to 40 per cent in 2000. The proportion of those who are not married for females aged 30-34 years was only 1 per cent in 1970, but it increased to 5 per cent in 1990, then to 11 per cent in 2000. The proportion of those who are not married for males aged 30–34 years increased from 6 per cent in 1970, to 14 per cent in 1990, and then to 28 per cent in 2000. The proportion of males aged 35–39 not married was only 1 per cent in 1970, but it increased 4 per cent in 1990, and then to 11 per cent in 2000.

Table 3.12. Trends of the proportion (by percentage) of those who are not married in Korea

Age group	1970	1980	1990	2000
Female				
20–24	57	66	81	89
25–29	10	14	22	40

30–34	1	3	5	11
Male				
20–24	93	93	96	98
25–29	43	45	57	71
30–34	6	7	14	28
35–39	1	2	4	11

Source: KNSO. Korea Statistical Yearbook. 2002.

Trends in population ageing

The rapid process of demographic transition has brought about an increase in both the absolute number and the proportion of the elderly in Korea. Those aged 60 and over increased from 1.5 million in 1960 to 3.3 million in 1990, and this number is projected to increase to 9.9 million by the year 2020 (Kim I K, 2004). This shows that the number of elderly people aged 60 years and over has doubled within the past three decades and is expected to increase by almost three times the 1990 figure and more than six times the 1960 figure.

Table 3.13 shows the age structure of the population from 1960 to 2000. The proportion of young people aged 0–14 years has continuously decreased. On the other hand, the proportion of the elderly aged 65 years and over has consistently increased over time: from 2.9 per cent in 1960, to 3.9 per cent in 1980, and then to 5.9 per cent in 1995. The proportion of those aged 65 years and over reached to 7.3 per cent in 2000, which indicates that Korea has become an 'ageing society'.

Table 3.13. Trends in the age structure of Korea, 1960–2000 (%)

Year	Total	0-14	15-64	65+	75+
1960	100.0	40.6	55.6	2.9	0.9
1966	100.0	43.5	53.2	3.3	0.9
1970	100.0	42.1	54.6	3.3	0.9

1975	100.0	38.1	58.4	3.5	1.0
1980	100.0	33.8	62.3	3.9	1.1
1985	100.0	29.9	65.7	4.3	1.3
1990	100.0	25.7	69.4	5.0	1.5
1995	100.0	23.0	71.1	5.9	1.9
2000	100.0	21.0	71.7	7.3	2.3

Source: KNSO (Population and Housing Census Report, each year).

Trends in the growth rate of each age group reveal a different pattern. Table 3.14 indicates these trends for the period from 1960 to 2000. The growth rate of the young population aged 0–14 years decreased but showed a positive rate from 1960 to 1970, and then from 1970 to 1975 it showed a zero growth rate. Since 1975, it has continuously shown a negative growth rate.

The proportion of those aged 15–64 years showed a higher growth rate than that of the elderly aged 65 years and over, until 1975. Since 1975, however, the proportion of this age group has shown lower growth rate than that of the elderly. This table also shows an interesting finding in that the proportion of those aged 75 years and over has been higher through all the years than that of those aged 65 years and over.

Table 3.14. Trends in the annual growth of the age structure in Korea, 1960–2000 (%)

Year	Total population	0–14	15–64	65 +	75 +
1960–1966	2.8	4.2	2.0	0.5	1.7
1966–1970	2.0	1.1	2.6	2.0	3.1
1970–1975	2.1	0.0	3.6	3.2	3.5
1975–1980	1.6	-0.8	3.0	4.0	3.7

1980–1985	1.6	-0.9	2.8	4.2	6.2
1985–1990	1.5	-1.6	2.6	4.7	5.4
1990–1995	0.5	-1.6	1.1	4.4	5.0
1995–2000	0.6	-1.2	0.8	5.6	5.9

Source: KNSO (Population and Housing Census Report, each year).

Table 3.15 shows Korea's projected population and population growth rates. The population is projected to increase up to 2020, and thereafter to decrease drastically. The proportion of the young population aged 0–14 years is projected to consistently decrease: from 21.1 per cent in 2000, to 13.9 per cent in 2020, and then to 10.5 per cent in 2050. The proportion of the working age group of 15–64 years is projected to increase from 71.7 per cent in 2000 to 72.1 per cent in 2010, and then consistently to decrease after 2010. In contrast to the other age groups, the proportion of the elderly aged 65 years and over is projected to continuously increase: from 7.3 per cent in 2000, to 15.1 in 2020, to 23.1 per cent in 2030, then to 34.4 per cent in 2050.

Table 3.15. Projected total population and population growth rates, 2000–2050 (Unit: 1000 persons, %)

	2000	2010	2020	2030	2040	2050
Total population	47,008	49,594	50,650	50,296	48,204	44,337
Annual pop growth rate	0.71	0.38	0.04	-0.24	-0.64	-1.04
Total	100.0	100.0	100.0	100.0	100.0	100.0
% Age 0–14	21.1	17.2	13.9	12.4	11.5	10.5
% Age 15–64	71.6	72.1	71.0	64.6	58.4	55.1
% Age 65+	7.3	10.7	15.1	23.1	30.1	34.4

Source: KNSO (2001).

Concluding remarks

This chapter has described the changes in Korea's demography since the 1960s. In addition to general trends in demographic transition, it has dealt with mortality transition, fertility transition, and the process of population ageing. Along with rapid economic development, Korea has experienced rapid demographic changes in urbanisation, significant declines in mortality and fertility and a significant rise in the age of its population.

Like many countries in the 21st century, Korea is faced with the serious demographic trends of very low fertility rates and a rapidly ageing population. In the early 1960s, concerned with rapid population growth, the Korean Government adopted national family planning programs. These programs are known to have been one of the most successful cases in the world in reducing a high fertility level. Less than 40 years later, however, the Korean Government is again worrying about the fertility level, but this time it is now one of the lowest in the world. As of 2004, the total fertility rate in Korea was reported to be 1.17.

Korea has experienced a very rapid decline in fertility, since the beginning of the 1960s. Because of this trend, both the UN and the KNSO predict that from 1995 to 2050 the population of working age people in Korea will drastically decrease (KNSO, 2001; United Nations, 2000). In relation to this drastic decline in the labour force, the UN suggests that encouraging immigration would be the only acceptable policy to cope with the labour shortage. As Korea has been experiencing below replacement rates of fertility since 1984, the rapid decline in fertility and the equally rapid ageing of the population have had substantial effects on Korea society. As there is no foreseeable shift in these trends, Korea will have to act quickly to address its population problems. Various adaptive mechanisms, such an increased migration to address the labour shortage, will be necessary.

References

Ban S H, 1977. The new community movement. In Kim C K, ed *Industrial and Social Development Issues*. Korea Development Institute, 1977, Seoul.

Choi, J.H. et al, 1993. *Causes and Consequences of Imbalanced Regional Distribution of Population.* [In Korean]. KNSO (Korea National Statistical Office)

Choi J H and Chang S H, 2003. Population distribution, internal migration and urbanization. In *The Population of Korea*. Population Association of Korea. KNSO (Korea National Statistical Office).

Coale A, 1973. The Demographic Transition. *International Population Conference*. Vol 1 Liege: International Union for the Scientific Stude of Population (IUSSP).

Cowgill D O, 1986. *Aging Around the World*. Belmont: Wadsworth.

Jun, K H, 2003. In *The Population of Korea*. KNSO (Korea National Statistical Office).

Kim D S, 2003. *Growth and transition in the population of Korea.* KNSO (Korea National Statistical Office)

Kim I K, 1987. *Socioeconomic Development and Fertility in Korea.* Seoul: Population and Development Studies Center, Seoul National University.

Kim I K, 1992. A Comparative Study of Demographic Transition between Korea and Japan. [In Korean]. *Dongguk Journal of Sociology*, 1, pp 43–78.

Kim I K, 2004. Different patterns of the living arrangements of the elderly in urban and rural Korea. Paper presented at the World Congress of Sociology in Beijing.

Kim T H, 2003. Mortality. In *The Population of Korea*. KNSO (Korea National Statistical Office).

KNSO – *see* Korea National Statistical Office.

Korea National Statistical Office, 2001. *Population Projections for Korea, 2000–2050*. KNSO (Korea National Statistical Office)

Korea National Statistical Office, 2002. *Social Indicators of Korea.*

Kwon T H et al, 1975. *The Population of Korea.* Seoul: Seoul National University Press.

Kwon T H, 1977. *Demography of Korea: Population Change and Its Components 1925–66*. Seoul: Population and Development Studies Center. Seoul: Seoul National University Press.

Lee H Y, 1980. Demographic Transition in Korea. *Bulletin of the Population and Development Studies Center*, 8, pp 5–17.

Lee J and Paik M, 2006. Sex Preferences and Fertility in South Korea During The Year of The Horse. *Demography*, Vol43, No 2, May 2006, pp 269–292.

Luther H U, 1979. Saemaul Undong: The modernization of rural poverty in South Korea. *Internationales Asienforum Internationales Asiani Foroum,* Vol 10, Nos 3/4, 1979, pp 329–358.

Moon S G, 1978. Urban-rural disparity in socioeconomic and demographic changes in Korea, 1960–1970. *Bulletin of the Population and Development Studies Center,* 7, pp 1–25.

United Nations, 2000. Below Replacement Fertility. *Population Bulletin of the United Nations*, United Nations Population Division.

4

The impact of new technologies on the digital generation: a critical analysis and review of policy making in Australia

Ali Mubarak

There has been a rapid increase in the use of digital technology within Australian households in the past decade. In 1998 only 41 per cent of Australian households had Internet access; in 2006 this figure had increased to 60 per cent (ABS, 2006). A further indicator of the rapid spread of up-to-date technology in Australia is the use of broadband connections. In 2005–06, the number of households with broadband Internet connections almost doubled to 2.3 million, reflecting the enthusiasm with which Australian homes have adopted Internet technology. A significant increase in Internet use among children is also evident. In 2006 nearly 92 per cent of children aged five to 14 years used a computer and 65 per cent used the Internet (ABS, 2006). Internet usage appeared to increase with age, from 37 per cent for 5–8 year olds to 88 per cent for 12–14 year olds. Increasing use of digital technology by young people has become an accepted norm in most Australian households.

Mobile phone technology is another important digital tool and plays a key role in the life of young people in Australia. According to the Australian Telecommunications Association mobile phone subscription was around 19 million at the end of 2006. Due to rapid advancement in broadband and mobile phone technology, the mobile phone industry has been constantly launching new features within mobile phones, tempting young people to buy them. It is now very common to see mobile phones carrying Internet-based technological tools, adding to the capacity for younger Australians to be the primary users of Internet technology.

In a survey completed in 2003, the 'Kids are calling' section of the McNair Ingenuity Research Australian Kids Consumer Insights, it was reported that:

> one in four children aged from six to 13 now have a mobile phone; more than 90 per cent of children aged from six to nine have used a mobile phone, usually one belonging to their parents; young girls are more likely to use a mobile phone than boys of the same age, and are significantly more likely to have their own mobile phone" (DCITA, 2005: 10)

This type of statistical detail effectively defines the digital generation. Young people born in the period from the early 1990s to 2000, aged somewhere between 7 years and 16 years are the 'digital generation' and will be the primary focus of this chapter.

In a 2006 report, the Internet Industry Association predicted that by the year 2010 average Australian household expenditure on digital entertainment products, voice calls and Internet would be $A300 per month. This report also predicted that broadband would have significantly increased young people's exposure to digital, home-based entertainment. Without doubt, the lifestyles of young people in Australia have gone through an enormous transformation due to new technologies that were not available to people born 30 years ago. Today Australia's younger generation is currently enjoying great advantages from increased access to entertainment and high speed communication
arising from digital technological tools. However, there is a dark side inherent in the risks that access to this technology creates. Given the state's long tradition of responsibility for the welfare of children and young people, the Australian Government is responding to the potentially harmful effects that might be experienced from such ready access to digital technological tools.

This chapter critically explores the social and psychological implications of digital technology on the digital generation within Australia. It also provides an overview of current and future policy directions to protect the interests of young people in Australia.

The social and psychological aspects of digital technological tools in relation to young people

Access to the Internet and mobile phone technologies have had wide social and economic effects on young people (Warden et al, 2004; Childnet International, 2006). While these modern technologies assist young people to be connected with their peer groups quickly and establish strong social support networks, they also pose some serious challenges to young people's security and wellbeing. Child abuse resulting from engagement with the Internet and Internet chat rooms, and the exposure of young people to pornographic and other offensive materials have been widely debated in recent years. Two significant issues stand out in these debates: sexual exploitation of children through the Internet (ECPAT, 2007), and the risk of creating psychological dependence and addiction among young people because the Internet acts as a powerful stimulant that provides instant feedback and excitement (Goldberg, 1996; West, 2001). Schwartz and Southern (2000) also argue that there is a strong possibility of people becoming psychologically addicted to using social interaction facilities on the Internet. In recent research it was found that nearly one third of adolescents appear to be compulsive Internet users (Mubarak, 2005); and psychiatrists Beard and Wolf (2001) suggest that Internet addiction is an impulse-control disorder requiring professional intervention.

The exposure of young people to sexually explicit or offensive materials online arose as a major concern in a recent study in Australia (Mubarack, 2005). The research found that almost half of 12–13 year olds reported accessing websites their parents would prefer them not to see and nearly half of the children reported exposure to inappropriate materials through pop-up windows and spam emails (ABA, 2005b). Flood and Hamilton (2003) also reported that children in Australia experience extensive exposure to pornography, with nearly 73 per cent of boys and 11 per cent of girls they interviewed reporting that they had watched sexually explicit videos online. Eighty-four per cent of boys and 60 per cent of girls reported that they had been exposed accidentally to sex sites on the Internet. Disturbingly, Mills (1998) observed that young people engaging in sexual activities via the Internet could not isolate their experiences from their real emotional lives; and Katelyn et al (2001) observed that those barred from expressing important sexual needs in their real life relationships were more likely to turn to the Internet to do so. The results of an online survey conducted among adolescent girls by Berson et al (2002) indicated that a significant number of these girls engaged in very risky behaviour when online and continued potentially problematic real life practices as a result of these interactions. Flood and Hamilton (2003) argue that children who are exposed to sexually explicit, violent and nude material are likely to become desensitised to a range of unacceptable behaviours, and it possibly encourages them into sexual abuse and exploitation.

There is also concern that language use within chat rooms is changing, exposing young people to further risk (Merchant's, 2001). Cyberspace is also serving as an alternative venue for forming relationships among adolescents who are alienated from their peers or parents, while more well-adjusted young people are less likely to engage in these interactions (Mitchell et al, 2003). A further finding is a marked decline due to high Internet use in civic engagement (individual and collective forms of action that are designed to identify and address matters of public concern) of young people (Putnam, 2000). Barrakat (2005) bemoans that online activities are eroding citizenship and fragmenting strengths in communities.

Mobile phones provide further challenges posed by the Internet. Due to broadband and 3G technology, access to the Internet via mobile phones has increased. The portability of Internet tools through mobile phones has significantly increased the exposure of children to unwanted materials on the Internet, such as pornography, sexual chat and commercial online chat services. In particular, the increased use of pre-paid phones has made it difficult to establish the age of mobile phone users. Easy availability of mobile phones at home has significantly increased the access of minors to unwanted materials on the Internet because they can often gain access without the need to enter passwords. Anti-social activities such as race hate messages, materials promoting violence, cults, drugs and eating disorders are easily passed on to a network of young people simultaneously by a click of a button through services such as instant messaging. Bullying has also emerged as a prevalent problem perpetrated through mobile phones.

Increasing debt for young people from big mobile phone bills has emerged as a major economic concern in recent years. For some young people, this results in increased stress due to poor financial management, often leading to excessive paid work that affects concentration at school (Childnet International, 2006). A further danger is that young people carry their private identity information such as name, telephone numbers and digital pictures of self and others on their mobile phone, which can be easily broken into. Complications arising from privacy issues have resulted in law enforcement processes becoming significantly more challenging for policing.

The functionality of mobile phones and other mobile communications devices has increased rapidly in Australia in recent years. These devices now deliver multimedia services, including audio-visual content and Internet services, which were once available only through a fixed environment. The 3G technology in particular has enhanced the capabilities of devices such as mobile phones, personal digital assistants and laptops with wireless connections, to provide advanced services such as: still image capture with mobile phones; video playback; Internet access; portal access to subscriber services; email functionality and; the features of hand held games consoles (DCITA, 2004). It is common in Australia to see service providers publicising the adult-themed services such as sex chat and pornography for adults, without having capacity to prevent these messages from reaching children.

Since mobile carriers have invested heavily in modern technology such as 3G in recent years, there has been strong competition in the Internet industry to invent innovative content and services. To meet such demands, the mobile carriers have established partnerships with many types of content providers. While the content currently available through mobile phones is deemed suitable to all audiences, some may include sexual content, violence and interactive gambling. These digitally led possibilities pose a serious challenge to policy makers in Australia in regulating the content of mobile phone carriers.

Thus, it is evident that while digital technology has been a wonderful gift to young Australians, it also poses many serious challenges to the welfare of children and young people who embrace it so willingly. It is crucial to safeguard the digital generation from the harm possible through new communications technology. The following section is an analysis of Australian policy making responses to these issues.

Policy making in the area of digital technology to protect the digital generation in Australia from harm

The Australian Government has shown a keen interest in protecting children and young people from the negative effects of new communications technology. Under Schedule 5 of the *Broadcasting Services Act 1992*, the Australian Government provided opportunities for the Internet industry to work together towards ensuring the safety of young people using digital technologies. This collaborative approach was refined further as the Internet industry transformed and advanced its capacities. During subsequent years, the Australian Government's Department of Communications, Information Technology and the Arts launched enquiries into the content of online bulletin boards. Based on its findings, it prepared a report on the regulation of online services in 1996. In the same year the Australian Broadcasting Authority (ABA) (now the Australian Communications and Media Authority, (ACMA) since July 2005) launched an inquiry into the content of Internet service providers (ISPs) and released a report titled 'Investigation into the content of online services'. This report proposed that a self-regulatory system be introduced in Australia in which the Internet industry would be guided by its voluntarily developed codes of practice and the ACMA's content rating scheme. Due to rapid developments occurring in the Internet industry, the Australian Government's Senate Select Sub-committee on Information Technologies was formed in 1998 and conducted its own inquiry covering a wide range of issues related to Internet content. This committee launched a self-regulatory mechanism through which the Australian Government and the Internet industry were to work together.

The *Broadcasting Services Amendment (online services) Act* was passed in 1999 and came into effect January 2000. According to this Act, the ABA was required to establish a complaints hotline for the community to notify the government of Internet content that is not suitable for children and younger people (Family and Community Development Committee, 2000). The Act also required the Internet industry to develop its own industry codes of practice and implementation on a voluntary basis. The ABA and Internet industry were also required to launch community education programs and raise awareness about child safety on the Internet.

Classification system of content available on the Internet in Australia

Classifying content available on Internet-based technology tools is a crucial task in protecting the digital generation from exposure to inappropriate material. The AMCA uses a co-regulatory scheme that came into effect in 1999, and sits within the National Classification Board (which was originally established to classify films and videotapes) to classify material available on the Internet. According to this classification system, material containing detailed instructions about how to conduct criminal acts, violence or drug use, child pornography,
bestiality, excessively violent or sexually violent materials, and actual depiction of sexual activity are rated as X or RC, and are totally banned. Material classified as R, which includes excessive violence or sexual violence, implied or simulated activity, and material suitable only for adults, can be viewed only by adults aged 18 years and over. This material is required to be filtered using advanced filtering technology so that only adults have access to it. The AMCA's classification system applies to all material originating from Australia. According to this classification system, the AMCA can direct an ISP or an Internet content host (ICH) to remove prohibited or potentially prohibited content from the Internet. If the

AMCA considers that certain content on the Internet poses a threat to any segment of society or is illegal, it will refer the matter to the police.

Material originating from overseas, produced outside the ACMA's jurisdiction, poses a major challenge. Details of prohibited content or content hosted outside Australia are forwarded to the makers or suppliers of the filter products, who are listed in the schedule of the registered code of practice for Internet service providers (ISPs) in Australia. On notification by the ACMA the makers or suppliers of these products are required to agree to make modifications to offensive content. The code also requires Australian ISPs to provide Internet filters to their subscribers that will protect the children and young people from exposure to material that is unsuitable for their age and maturity (ABA, 2005a).

Community education on digital media

As per the *above mentioned regulations*, the ACMA and the Internet Industry Association (IIA) are obligated to establish a close rapport with the community and create channels through which community members can provide feedback on the content available on the Internet. The ACMA has created a community education wing, known as NetAlert (ACMA, 2005), with its own website that provides useful information about the regulation of online content. It creates community awareness about online content that is harmful to the community. This website also has tools to help the community provide feedback to the ACMA about online content. NetAlert has established close links with local city councils, libraries, state and territory education departments and academic institutions to disseminate useful information related to the cyber media, and the ABA's fight against the challenges posed by digital media.

The IIA has also created its own community education program through its website, which provides up-to-date information on Internet filters and other digital technological tools available in the market. It also evaluates their advantages and disadvantages. The updated version of the Internet industry codes of practice contains useful information on legal issues pertaining to online content and the community's role in providing feedback and complaints to the IIA. My search through the Internet revealed the presence of many other Australian-hosted websites that provide information to young people and their parents about safety on the Internet. These include SimGuard, Cybersmart Kids, CyberAngels, Young Media Australia, Parents Guide to the Internet, Netmom, National Centre for Missing and Exploited Children, Safe Teens, Centre for Media Education, Smartparent and Netparents, all helpful in creating awareness about content available on the Internet. The presence of so many information sites also emphasises the level of risk that children and young people face in digital technology environments.

The Internet industry codes of practice

In response to government regulation, the Australian Internet industry has created its own codes of practice. The codes provide guidelines for members of the Australian based Internet Industry Association (IIA) to ensure the protection of children from inappropriate content. In particular, the government requires ISPs to monitor content available online and the IIA to revise its Internet industry codes of practice annually. The IIA must also provide all necessary information to the community about technological developments occurring and how communities can benefit from them. In a 2005 review, the IIA fully endorsed the need for developing technological solutions for managing children's use of the Internet. This code of practice *encourages* the ISPs or ICHs to use appropriate warnings and/or labelling systems to warn minors that the content is intended for adults only. This includes material that is potentially prohibited. The code of practice also requires the ISPs or ICHs to take necessary steps to make sure that material available on their services is not in contravention of any Australian state, territory or federal law. The IIA also stresses that each ISP or ICH will, upon notification from the ACMA that certain newsgroups are linked with child pornography and paedophile activity, take *reasonable* steps to ensure that its newsreaders' server will not accept feeds from such newsgroups.

The latest industry codes of practice require Internet service providers to take reasonable steps to inform their end users about the methods of supervising and managing children's access to Internet content, and about the availability of one or more IIA family friendly filters and how they can be obtained. They must also provide a list of one or more IIA family friendly filters with links to effect download and instructions for use. These codes of practice insist that content providers ensure that the community is informed about, and assisted in providing feedback to the AMCA about the content hosted within the Internet by the ISPs and ICHs. In order to achieve this objective, the IIA has suggested that content providers create an online Safety Page by providing a direct hyperlink (an online safety button) to the IIA's Safety Page that will help members of the community provide feedback.

Challenges posed by law enforcement in relation to Internet and mobile content in Australia

It is evident from the above discussion that Australia has shown keen interest in protecting children and young people from the potential harm of the Internet. However, there remain serious challenges in enforcing policies due to the fact that the Internet transcends national boundaries and many forces outside Australia contribute to the available content. Keeping this in mind, there has been increased inter-country collaboration in recent years, to attempt to address the challenges at hand. Many industrially advanced countries have started cooperating in matters relating to law enforcement on sex offences pertaining to children. This trend has forced Australia to work closely with law enforcement agencies overseas so the Australian High Tech Crime Centre was created. This body has established ties with 18 international law enforcement agencies, which include Interpol, the Internet Hotline Providers Association (INHOPE) and the Cyber Tip Line.

However, this trend is not common to all countries in the world, creating a major obstacle for law enforcement in Australia. For example, law enforcement on inappropriate Internet content is not uniform in countries such as Russia, India and China. In 2003–04 more than 99 per cent of prohibited Internet content investigated by the ABA was hosted overseas and approximately 65 per cent was sufficiently serious to warrant immediate action. In the same year, the

ABA referred more than 700 items of prohibited overseas-hosted content to filter manufacturers listed in the codes of practice so that access to such content would be blocked by users of those filters (ABA, 2005c).

The Australian High Tech Crime Centre has also been playing a pivotal role in coordinating joint law enforcement operations involving all states and federal law enforcement authorities within Australia. In 2001, the Australian Cyber Crime Act was amended to add a new section (3LA) to the Crimes Act 1914 (Commonwealth), which means law enforcement officers now have the power to compel a person to reveal their private encryption keys, and personal identification numbers or passwords, thus enabling the officers, for the purpose of investigation, to access information held on a computer.

In 2004, the Australian National Ethical Offenders Register was launched by the Australian Government. This requires all state and territory governments to notify the public of personal details, addresses and travel plans of people convicted of some serious offences involving children. In the same year, the government also enacted the *Crimes Legislation Amendment (Telecommunications Offences and other measures) Act (No 2) 2004* which came into effect in March 2005. This amendment to the Act was made to protect children from sexual exploitation. The Act declares that it is a criminal offence under Commonwealth law to use the Internet or any telecommunications service or device to access, possess, send, cause to be sent, make available, publish or distribute child pornography materials or child abuse material. This law in particular has increased the responsibilities of ISPs and ICHs for the protection of children and young people.

In order to enforce the law effectively to protect the interests of children, the government has created the Australian Federal Police Online Child Sex Exploitation Team (OCSET). This team performs an investigative and coordination role within Australia for multi-jurisdictional and international online child sex exploitation matters. This crime investigation wing has been given the important responsibility of investigating matters related to online child exploitation, including pornography, abuse, grooming and procurement of children. These matters include those referred from Australian state and territory police, government and non-government organisations (including ISPs and ICHs), the Australian High Tech Crime Centre, international law enforcement agencies, Interpol and members of the public. The Australian Federal Police can investigate Internet sites carrying offensive material that are operated from an ISP within Australia. Any sites not within Australia are referred to overseas law enforcement agencies. The Australian Federal Police reports that OCSET has been functioning effectively, as evidenced by a number of arrests. During 2005–06, 21,781 child pornography images and 416 movies were located on the Internet, resulting in the investigation of the persons and organisations responsible (AFP, 2006).

The Australian Government continues to show its ongoing interest and leadership qualities in trying to improve the digital generation's safety online. In June 2006, the Department of Communications, Information Technology and the Arts announced the government's intention to create a National Filter Scheme to provide every Australian family with a free Internet filter as part of a $116.6 million comprehensive package of measures to crack down on Internet pornography. This scheme also aimed to provide libraries with free filters so that computers in libraries across Australia would also become child-friendly. As part of this scheme, NetAlert, launched a comprehensive national community education campaign to ensure that all Australian parents were aware of the benefits of regulating their children's Internet experience by using a safe and effective computer filter. However, although filtering technology has proved very useful in protecting children against prohibited Internet content, Australian families do not seem to be installing Internet filters in their home computers. The ABA (2005b) survey revealed that a proper filter was installed in only 35 per cent of Australian households. This survey seems to reflect parents' 'trust' that their children will self-censor, rather than taking the firm step of installing filters. This trend clearly indicates that Australian households are yet to understand the importance of installing Internet filters on their home computers. To overcome this situation, the Australian Government is exploring the possibility of introducing online content filters at the ISP end. Recently, the ACMA launched a series of trials of ISP-based filtering. However, NetAlert reports that filtering online content at the ISP level leads to a significant reduction in the speed and efficiency of ISP computer networks and that ISPs will be confronted with serious technical challenges if ISP–level filtering is introduced. It further argues that the existing co-regulatory scheme, with its strong focus on using community education to encourage Australian families to install Internet filters at home will be of greater benefit than introducing filtering at the ISP level (NetAlert, 2006).

Yet another policy direction currently under consideration by the Australian Government is the possibility of introducing restrictions on online content hosted by overseas ISPs that is classified 'R' (adults only). It has been argued that a high proportion of adults would opt out of a filtering system that blocks R rated content from overseas sites because this content includes a wide range of material that, though it may be harmful to children, does not harm adults. Such a policy decision would be a major step toward protecting the children and young people from the harmful effects of digital media. However, this policy involves wider issues such as which themes are harmful to children, who will decide which content is harmful, and who will enforce prohibition on content originating from overseas.

Outcomes of law enforcement in Australia for protecting the digital generation from harm

A six-month report published in 2005 on the online content co-regulatory scheme showed that the ACMA's Internet Complaints Hotline received 451 complaints, including 46 invalid complaints (ACMA, 2005b). Of these, 82 investigations were terminated due to the ACMA being unable to locate the Internet content referred to by the complainant. The ACMA completed 318 investigations, 222 (70 per cent) of which resulted in the location of prohibited Internet content. The report also indicates that the ACMA investigated 398 prohibited items of Internet content and found that 323 items (80 per cent) were 'Refused Classification' (RC). Of these, 272 (84 per cent) contained exploitative/offensive depictions of children or were otherwise related to paedophilia. The report found that a majority of prohibited items of Internet content were hosted overseas. More than half the content was hosted from the United States. Europe accounted for 23 per cent, with a significant proportion coming from Russia and China. South Korea and Hong Kong accounted for approximately 13 per cent. This report clearly indicates the enormity of the situation in protecting children living in the digital era.

In a recent study on the experiences of young people interacting through the Internet, based on focus group discussions among 114 high school students in the 13–17 years age group, it was found that young people spent nearly 13 hours per week accessing the Internet and approximately one third of them were likely to have a psychological addiction to its use (Mubarak, 2005). Only 18 per cent of young people reported parental support and guidance for Internet use. This research also suggested a gender-biased parental attention to the use of Internet in that 39 per cent of the parents of female respondents had shown concern or objections to chat room use, but only seven per cent of the parents of male respondents had shown concern or objections to their chat room use.

Such research indicates that messages about protecting the digital generation have not reached Australian communities. While the digital generation is busy enjoying the benefits of digital tools, simultaneously they are at risk of being seriously affected by these tools' negative effects. This situation poses a serious question about the effectiveness of the current self-regulatory scheme for filtering Internet content and of the Australian Government's initiative to promote community awareness about the safety of children online.

A reason for the weakness of 'voluntary' self-regulation by the Internet industry could be the conflict between ISP business interests and their moral responsibility toward the welfare of the community. The conflict of interest within the IIA is evident from its recently launched Responsible Business Program. One can see many phrases such as 'take reasonable steps', 'provide reasonable assistance', 'ensure the best possible', being used in the guidelines for the ISPs and ICHs. Obviously these phrases leave to the individual service provider the final decision as to the extent to which it will take responsibility.

While the Australian Government's initiative to introduce compulsory filters at ISP level is a healthy move, it is also necessary for the Internet industry to take more responsibility in reducing potential harm for children and young people online. This may require the introduction of certain specific guidelines by the government, which must be followed strictly by the Internet industry. In other words, I am suggesting that the existing regime of self-regulation needs to be replaced with a government-regulated or quasi-regulated system. While the government's recent proposal to introduce compulsory filters at ISP level is promising, it has many technical hurdles to overcome. It is important that the Internet industry share the costs involved in promoting the safety of the digital generation. Similarly, the level of success achieved by the government's community education program needs to be evaluated critically. Based on the observations reported by the Australian Government (ABA, 2005b) and my own research, it is evident that the community has not been educated sufficiently to make all reasonable efforts to protect the children and young people from the possibly negative effects of available digital technology.

Conclusion

Without any doubt the rapid expansion of the digital technological world has the potential to empower the digital generation. It is important that we acknowledge the enormous benefits that digital technology has brought to young people who have been left behind for many decades. In particular, children from poor families, young people with disabilities and children from remote areas of Australia such as Aboriginal communities have benefited a lot by being brought into the mainstream with new technologies. Today, it is very common to see such groups in the Australian community actively chatting with the world community, overcoming the barriers that they had for many generations, thanks to the simplicity and cost effectiveness of new technological tools such as the Internet and mobile phones.

However, with the advantages of digital technology come many challenges such as those that have been discussed in this chapter. It is obvious from recent research that it has taken more than a decade for Australia and, to some extent, the whole world to understand the enormity of challenges the digital technological tools have brought with them. Without doubt these challenges will increase with the rapidity with which the digital world is expanding. Australian policy-makers have made it clear in their statements that law enforcement to protect children and young people online will not be successful without the active participation of Australian families and communities. The challenge in the future lies in the extent to which more coordinated strategies involving all segments of Australian communities are developed to protect current and future digital generations from risk of harm in what is an increasingly integral part of their daily existence.

References

ABA – *see* Australian Broadcasting Authority

ABS – *see* Australian Bureau of Statistics

AFP – *see* Australian Federal Police

ACMA – see Australian Communications and Media Authority

Australian Broadcasting Authority, 2005a. Five years on: Internet content regulation in review, *ABA Update* (138).

Australian Broadcasting Authority, 2005b. Kidsonline @ home - Inernet use in Australian homes, Australian Broadcasting Authority and netAlert Limited, Commonwealth of Australia, Sydney, Australia.

Australian Broadcasting Authority, 2005c. Six month report on the online content co-regulatory scheme – Reporting period from 10 July to December 2004, Australian Broadcasting Authority, Commonwealth, Canberra, Australia.

Australian Broadcasting Authority, 2006. Six month report on the online content co-regulatory scheme, Reporting period 12 July to December 2005, Commonwealth, Canberra, Australia.

Australian Communications and Media Authority (ACMA), 2005. Internet Safety Needs Highlighted as Cyber Survey Reveals Kids Are online Younger and Longer. Press Release, Australian Communications and Media Authority website, Canberra, Australian Government. http://www.acma.gov.au/ WEB/STANDARD//pc=PC_91688.

Australian Bureau of Statistics, 2006. Internet activity, Australia, Report No. 8153.0, Australian Bureau of Statistics, Canberra.

Australian Federal Police, 2006. Australian Federal Police Annual Report 2005 -06, Commonwealth of Australia, Canberra, Australia.

Barrakat J, 2005. Online opportunities for civic engagement? An examination of Australian third sector organisations on the Internet. *Australian Journal of Emerging Technologies and Society*, 3 (1), pp 18–30.

Beard K & Wolf E, 2001. Modification in the proposed diagnostic criteria for Internet addiction. *CyberPsychology and Behavior*, 4, pp 377–383.

Berson R I, Berson M J and Ferron J M, 2002. Emerging risks of violence in the digital age: Lessons for educators from an online study of adolescent girls in the Unites States. *Meridian: A middle school computer technologies journal* [online], 5 (2). Available from: http://www.ncsu.edu/meridian/sum2002/cyberviolence/8.html [accessed 03 April 2004].

Childnet International, 2006. www.childnet-int.ord [accessed on 26 March 2007].

DCITA – *see* Department of Communications, Information Technology and the Arts.

Department of Communications, Information Technology and the Arts, 2004. *Review of the operation of schedule 5 to the Broadcasting Services Act 1992*. Canberra: Commonwealth of Australia.

Department of Communications, Information Technology and the Arts, 2005. The social impact of mobile phone use in Australia: a review of data sources. Communications Research Uni, Canberra, Australian Government.

http://www.dcita.gov.au/communications_and_technology/publications_and_reports/2005/april/the_social_impact_of_mobile_phone_use_in_australia_a_review_of_data_sources.

ECPAT (End Child Prostitution and Trafficking), 2007. Available from: http://www.ecpat.net [accessed 26 March 2007].

Family and Community Development Committee, 2000. Inequality into the effects of television and multimedia on children and families in Victoria, Family and Community Development Committee, Melbourne, Victoria.

Flood and Hamilton C, 2003. Regulating youth access to pornography, Discussion Paper No. 53, The Australian Institute, Manuka ACT, Australia.

Goldberg I, 1996. Internet addiction disorder, Quoted by Warden N L, Phillips G & Ogloff RP, Internet addiction, Psychiatry, Psychology and Law, Volume 11 (2): 280 – 295, 2004.

Internet Industry Association, 2006. Year 2010 National broadband targets – maintaining Australia's competitiveness, Internet Industry Association, Manuka ACT, Australia.

Katelyn Y A, Green A S and Smith P K, 2001. Demarginalizing the Sexual Self. *The Journal of Sex Research*, 38 (4), pp 302–312.

Merchant G, 2001. Teenagers in cyberspace: an investigation of language use and language change in Internet chat rooms. *Journal of Research in Reading*, 24 (3), pp 293–254.

Mills R, 1998. Cyber: sexual chat on the Internet, *Journal of Popular Culture*, 32 (3), pp 31–47.

Mitchell K J, Finkelhor D and Wolak J, 2003. The exposure of young to unwanted sexual materials on the Internet: A national survey of risk, impact and prevention. *Young and Society*, 34 (3), pp 330–358.

Mubarak A R, 2005. A study of the friendship and social interaction facilities available on the Internet and their impact on adolescents. *Report submitted to the Faculty of Social Sciences, Flinders University, Adelaide*, Australia.

Net Alert (2006) Education the best filter for young Australians on the Internet, Media release available at: http://www.netalert.net.au/03004 - Education-the-best-Filter-for-young-Australians-on-the-Internet.asp [accessed 26 March 2007].

Putnam R, 2000. *Bowling alone: The collapse and revival of American community*. New York: Simon and Schuster.

Schwartz M F and Southern S, 2000. Compulsive cybersex: The new tea room. In Cooper A, ed *Cybersex: The dark side* of the force, A special issue of the Journal of sexual addiction & compulsivity, Philadelphia. Brunner Routledge, 2000, pp 127 – 144.

Warden N L, Phillips, J G and Ogloff R P, 2004. Internet addiction. *Psychiatry, Psychology and Law*, 11 (2), pp 280–295.

West R, 2001. Theories of Addiction. *Addiction*, 96, pp 3–13.

5

Participation, young people and the Internet: digital natives in Korea

Heejin Lee, Gil-Soo Han, Sangjo Oh

Introduction

The significance of Information and Communication Technology (ICT) has become critical in every facet of contemporary life and work. The coming of the Internet was no longer than two decades ago, but it has become a vital technology for all generations. Similar to the current trend towards 'the visual extravaganza' by newspaper and television (Barnhurst, 1998: 202), the Internet offers and utilises visual effects in an interactive and dynamic fashion. Moreover, individual users of the Internet are greatly empowered by the opportunity to participate interactively in public debate by airing their views online. Such an opportunity has brought about new avenues for citizens to participate in civic activities and influence political affairs and parties. Undoubtedly, the ways people use the Internet vary depending on their socioeconomic status and the generation to which they belong. Furthermore, the increasing penetration of the Internet opens up new avenues for political parties to attract public attention, especially when young people are increasingly losing interest in most news and information media, whilst gaining significant interest in the Internet (Barnhurst, 1998: 204).

In this chapter we examine how the Internet has affected the public and political participation of young people. We present two case studies where groups of secondary school students from South Korea have appealed to their basic human rights in order to influence policy decisions that had the potential to reduce their quality of life at school. The cases are indicative of the kind of opportunities available to develop innovative ways of participating in the political process. It is a common assumption that young people's increasing preoccupation with computers and the Internet has resulted in their loss of interest in social and political affairs. These two case studies, however, from a country that enjoys the most advanced Internet infrastructure in the world, demonstrate that this common perception is an inaccurate generalisation.

In the next section, we review studies on the impacts of computers and the Internet on the political participation of younger generations. This is followed by a description of Korean society characterised as 'the Internetworked society'. The two case studies are then examined, followed by a discussion of their main implications. We conclude with an assessment of the wider implications for politicians, policy-makers and civil society activists and provide suggestions for further research.

Whither civic participation in the Internet era?

Researchers have questioned whether online communication by the so-called 'digital generation' would sustain local networks or develop more distant relationships between people. It is a common perception that technological advancements, in particular computers and the Internet, have led to young people losing interest and initiative in participating in politics and engaging in social activities. For example, at home, the younger members of the family can often be found in their rooms, surfing the Net, and chatting and playing games online. Their preoccupation with ICTs and their close connection with members of the virtual world or cyberspace (i.e. online communities) the argument goes, may have the effect of depriving young people of face-to-face interpersonal skills required for interacting with 'real' members of society (i.e. 'offline' communities). As a result, young people tend to be complacent within their virtual world and become citizens indifferent to political participation.

Such observations are championed by Robert Putnam (1995, 2000), who blames TV as the main culprit of the marked decline in civic engagement in the United States. Putnam (1995: 67) argues that there has been a significant erosion of civic participation – an essential part of the liveliness and robustness of American society – or social capital. In his words, "features of social organization such as networks, norms, and social trust that facilitate co-ordination and co-operation for mutual benefit" decrease due to high engagement with TV. This argument could apply equally to the effects of the Internet.

Recent studies, however, show that a decrease in social participation cannot be attributed solely to the prevalent use of the Internet. Livingstone et al (2005) argue that young people are using the Internet for a wide range of activities that could be considered participatory. They suggest that 'political' participation be broadly defined to include interests not only in party politics and government policies, but also in civic and social activities to do with the environment, animal rights, anti-globalisation, gay rights and community activism (Livingstone et al, 2005, 288). Adopting this broader definition, many are optimistic about the potential contribution of the Internet to young people's political participation (Hall & Newbury, 1999; Bentivegna, 2002). The Internet is perceived to be a useful technology for stimulating democratic participation by the masses, enabling citizens to be engaged in political matters (Katz et al, 2001; Rice & Katz, 2004).

Therefore, the popular view that links the consequences of young people's engagement with the Internet to a decline in their social interactions may be overly simplistic. This view tends to overlook the fact that younger generations brought up with the Internet – often called digital natives (Prensky, 2001) – are different from older generations in the way they interact with other members of society or engage in political activities (Livingstone & Bober, 2005). For example, Livingstone and Bober (2005: 3) found that "54% of 12–19 year olds who use the Internet at least weekly have sought out sites concerned with political or civic issues." This proportion is significant by any means of measurement.

Barnhurst (1998: 211) describes how major media outlets like TV can change and mould young people's views about starving children in poor nations and inform them about the types of political action required to help out. The Internet may readily provide young people with such information too. The Internet facilitates peer-to-peer connection at a low cost – not only financially but also cognitively – by providing the information needed to participate in society. While maintaining this peer-to-peer connection, young people find it necessary to go beyond consuming the content provided for them by others and to seek out, select and judge content, even create content for themselves, as a member of a community. This broader approach stimulates interests that may lead to the pursuit of goals that reflect the traditional political agenda (Livingstone et al, 2005).

However, Livingstone's study was conducted in the United Kingdom and although the Internet, and more importantly broadband Internet, is widely available in Britain, it is reasonable to assume that the easier the access to fast Internet and the lower the price of Internet service, the easier it is to observe how young people behave in online environments. The following cases in Korea, with its advanced broadband networks, can therefore provide us with important insights into what could happen in the future in the context of advanced communications infrastructures.

The 'Internetworked' society: South Korea

Korea has the highest penetration of broadband in the world (Figure 5.1). The number of broadband subscribers in Korea reached 11 million in mid-2003 (Figure 5.2), with about 77 per cent of 14.3 million homes connected at a speed of over 2 Mbps. What is more astonishing is that all this was achieved in less than four years from the introduction of the first broadband services in July 1998.

Figure 5.1. Broadband access in OECD countries per 100 inhabitants

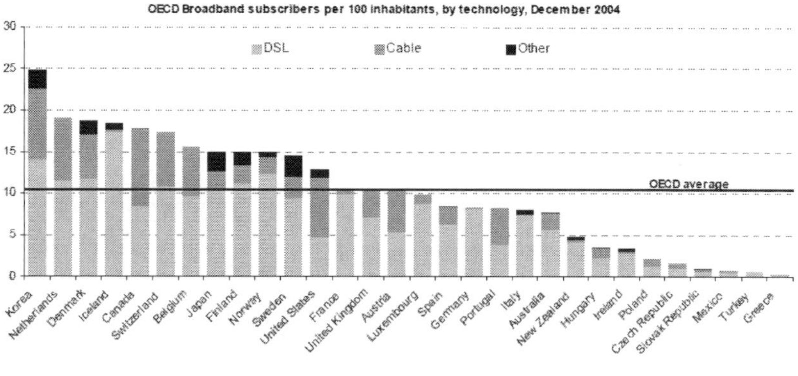

Source: OECD, 2005.

The widespread availability of broadband has significantly transformed the way Koreans use the Internet and live their lives (Lee et al, 2003). In terms of the number of Internet users per 100 inhabitants, Korea with 61.07 per cent in 2003 (ITU, 2007) has the third highest ratio after Iceland (67.47) and Sweden (63.00). With broadband Internet deeply embedded in everyday life, Koreans perceive it as a necessity, a facility they take for granted. It has become such a critical part of their lives that the Internet had a decisive impact on the result of the presidential election in 2002 (Guardian, 2003; Kim et al, 2004). Contemporary Korean society is thus characterised by its high connectivity, through broadband Internet and increasingly through mobile Internet. We therefore call it an 'Internetworked society'.

Figure 5.2. Number of broadband Internet subscribers in Korea

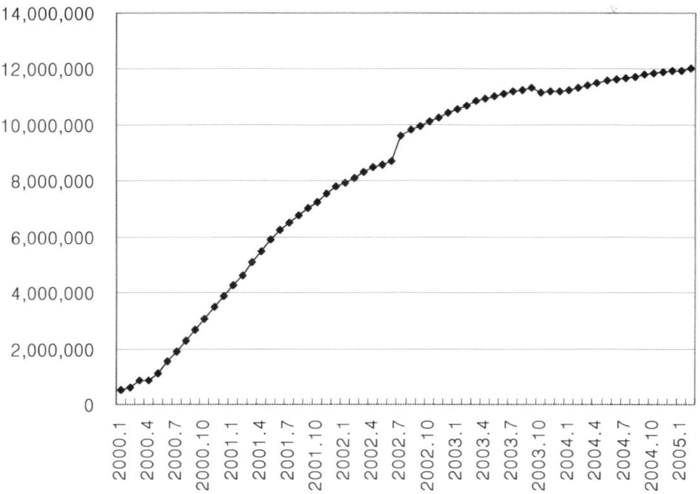

Source: National Internet Development Agency of Korea, 2006

The rapid roll-out and take-up of broadband services in Korea have been achieved through a combination of several factors: facilities-based competition, government leadership, geography and demographics, the PC Bang[1] phenomenon, pricing, and some unique elements of Korean culture.[2]

Two case studies: campaigns by young people

In the following section we present two examples where teenagers raised their voices collectively in the cause of human rights and protested against educational policies that would affect their quality of life at high school.

'No Cut' campaign

This campaign was concerned with the rigid hairstyle controls imposed in Korean secondary schools. Strict restrictions are placed on the appearance of students' hair, in particular its length. When a student is discovered with longer hair than allowed, the punishment is embarrassing. A hair razor is applied ruthlessly to create a line, or patch, of short hair through the long hair. Students call it 'a motorway is open'. Apart from creating an ugly look, it is a humiliating experience.

A group of students raised the haircut issue from a human rights perspective via a community website in May 2000. A further site dedicated to the haircut issue was also established at (http://idoo.net/?menu=nocut&sub=campaign). The 'No Cut' campaign grew both in the cyber world, where 1.6 million young people 'signed on' in support of the campaign in just three months, and on the street, where demonstrations were successfully organised. In October of that same year, the Ministry of Education announced a

---

[1] PC Bang (meaning "room" in Korean) is similar to Internet cafés in other countries. However, PC Bangs are perhaps a unique Korean phenomenon in terms of its popularity and impact in early years of broadband diffusion.

[2] Discussions of the success factors are beyond the scope of the paper. For details, see Lee and Choudrie (2002), Lee et al (2003), and Choudrie and Lee (2004).

recommendation that advised secondary schools to take a flexible approach on the matter (Donga Ilbo, 2000). However, the notorious practices continued; there was a reactionary movement by educators; student leaders and participants in the campaign were expelled from some schools; and the former restrictions were re-established.

In 2005, the 'No Cut' campaign was renewed under the banner of the 'National Network for the Protection of Student Human Rights' in which not only students but also citizen groups participated. This originally online network also organised offline demonstrations (Donga Ilbo, 2005). In response, the Minister of Education met with student representatives. (This is unprecedented in Korea, where secondary school students' demands are normally ignored along with the cause of university entrance exams. A typical saying is, "Persevere and survive your hellish secondary years, then the heavenly university life will come" – which is related to the second campaign below.) Although there was no tangible outcome from this meeting, it was a pleasing outcome and an achievement for the students who participated in the campaign because the Ministry responded in a serious manner.

Protest against the new university entrance selection scheme

The second case study concerns the protest against a newly introduced policy for university entrance exams. In October 2004 the Ministry of Education announced a new policy for the university entrance selection system which would come into effect for entry in 2008 and which therefore would affect the then Year 10 students at the time of the protest in early 2005.

The major change proposed increased weightings of academic grades across all subjects studied during the three years of high school, compared to the previous system of giving greater weightings to grades in the final year and the results of the national examination (equivalent to Victorian Certificate of Education in Victoria or High School Certificate in New South Wales of Australia).

In Korean society, going to a university, or more accurately speaking, going to a reputable or the 'best' university, is a major goal for almost every student. The new policy meant that students would have to work much harder throughout all three years of high school since all activities are assessed and, in theory, contribute to the final university entrance grade. In response to this proposal, many online communities (e.g. café.daum.net/freeHS) emerged, where high school students, mainly in Year 10, discussed and complained about the new policy (Yonhap News, 2005a). Through these online communities and SMS messaging, students also organised candlelight demonstrations, which attracted huge attention from the media and the general public (Yonhap News, 2005b).

What should be noted from both of these campaigns is the fact that all activities were initiated and organised through the Internet. Evidently the campaigns emerged because students initially expressed their anger in small online communities, and the presence of the communities was then circulated as a dedicated website. The sites attracted attention and became populated by a huge number of sympathetic students. It was on these sites that spontaneous suggestions for offline demonstrations were made by some community members. Once a suggestion was well received by the community, it was put into action, reflecting an organic form of democracy or cyber citizenship.

Discussion

Politicians in many countries, including Australia, are concerned that young people are increasingly losing interest in politics, civic participation, and social and community activities. However, the examples discussed above show that young people are still willing to participate when participation is in keeping with their virtual or digital activities, and action is in their interests. Undoubtedly the availability of various types of participation, and the opportunities for voices to be heard, are signs of a healthy society, both now and in the future.

As mentioned earlier, there are two opposing views as to whether there is a positive correlation between ICT and young people's participation in civic affairs. Although it is acknowledged that this area requires further research, three key implications arising from the case studies are discussed below.

First, today's generation is the first to have grown up with the Internet and mobile technologies. This is the generation Prensky (2001) calls 'digital natives', as opposed to 'digital immigrants' who are people in their 30s and over who entered the new digital age in mid-life. 'Digital natives' think and process information fundamentally differently from older generations. They are 'native speakers' of the digital language of computers, video games, the Internet and mobile phones. Their ways of expressing themselves, interacting and participating are different from those of 'digital immigrants'. They should not, therefore, be judged by the standards of 'digital immigrants'. 'Digital natives' may have, or may develop, their own way of participating in social and political activities. Further, the Internet and other information and communication technologies offer the digital natives new ways and motivations in carrying out their tasks (Carpini, 2000: 348). However, 'digital natives' as future leaders still need to work with digital immigrants in collaboration in terms of the issues and contexts that are yet to come rather than those of the past (Youniss et al, 2002).

This generation of young people tends to combine participation in social and political affairs with fun (Friedland & Morimoto, 2006). They use parody, humour, wit and caricature to express their feelings and opinions, rather than direct criticism. They may sometimes become 'flash' mobs: a demonstration is organised via mobile phone and the Internet; participants gather and display their message in an unusual, notable and often humorous way, just for a while; and then they quickly disperse. We need to find ways to encourage the digital generation's participation, nurture their political curiosity, and help them engage in social affairs (Coleman, 2004, 2005).

Finally, when we evaluate the social and political effects of technology on young people, we also need to see beyond the immediately obvious in their behaviour. Superficial assessment of young people's Internet-related behaviour may be less than productive. While they are pursuing fun and pleasure, it seems that they are not considering the broader social and political implications of their actions. However, based on the activities described above, their actions do not occur in a vacuum.

Their acts, including any type of Internet activities, necessarily involve goods and services, for example, computers, infrastructure and broader service networks. Thus, their engagement in the Internet results in intended or unintended consequence, e.g. support for the service networks and providers, which is closely tied to socio-economic dimensions of a given society. This engagement has political implications in itself, either intended or unintended. Therefore, we suggest that holding the perspective that young people who spend much of their time to the Internet are largely disengaged from politics has the potential to exacerbate any existing disengagement, by systematically dismissing their political opinions and participation and failing to acknowledge any interest. This view is rather simplistic as argued in this paper. To put this differently, individual agents' thoughts and actions ought to be influenced by or reflect existing social and economic structures. In turn, it is individual actions that transform the social and economic structures (Danermark et al, 1997; Bhaskar, 1989). However, it will take time until we realize the full implications of a new perspective or revolutionary medium such as the Internet on broader society.

Conclusion

There is a popular view that computers and the Internet tend to make young people less responsive to social or political demands of the society in which they live. Some studies (see Carpini, 2000) show however, that if we adopt a broader concept of participation, new media channels can in fact help young people to participate in civil activities by lowering the costs of participation. The two campaigns by young Koreans discussed in this chapter exemplify how the Internet can provide them with avenues to express desires and perspectives, and consequently facilitate their civic participation.

There are some important messages here for politicians, policy-makers and civil society groups. Those who are interested in young people need to consider new and innovative ways to reach this and future generations. The commonly proposed distinction between

'politicised' or digitally 'de-politicised' young people can be seen as an ill-informed and counter-productive perspective. As the significance of the Internet increases, patterns of political participation will continue to change. The era of the Internet has just begun and we still do not know the extent to which it will continue to influence people's everyday thinking and behaviour as well as broader governance issues. We need to think strategically and understand how to mobilise young people's creativity in a socially constructive way. This
will be an important question for a healthy democratic society in the future.

This chapter is not without its limitations. First of all, this chapter is built on two cases that are anecdotal, but could have been investigated in more detail. Although they are sufficient enough to show a trajectory of the relationship between youth and emerging new media, we still need more documentation of other convincing cases. Related to the first point, the examples we have presented in this chapter are from Korea, which has a unique socio-political context and history. It would be inappropriate to presume that the same level of advanced communication infrastructure in other societies will necessarily lead to a similar level of social participation among both young people and adults. Other societies may explore and encourage new and different ways to participate in social and political activities. For example, Lim Kit Siang, the opposition leader of Malaysia, has managed to attract much more serious interest than in the past from young Malaysians through his blog <http://blog.limkitsiang.com>. Similarly, the Australian Liberal Party launched the site (http://sameoldlabor.com) a parody critical of the opposition party, on the day when their rivals, the Australian Labor Party, elected a new leader; the site features a short and colourful animation which is highly accessible to youth. Moreover, how youth in countries with a long tradition of democracy (e.g. India) or an increasingly strong economic capacity (e.g. China) will express their political interest is yet to be seen. Iran is another interesting example. According to recent research (reported in USTODAY.com, 2005): "Although the Internet has not altered the power structure of the government [in Iran], it has transformed campaigning and laid the groundwork for political change." The report makes specific reference to how young people in Iran actively seek to have their political voice heard.

Further research is required to investigate the effects of emerging media on young people's social and political engagement in various social, cultural and political milieux. Such research will help provide a deeper understanding of the nature of political participation in the Internet Age. This will also enlighten future directions for so-called 'digital democracy' and 'e-politics'.

References

Barnhurst K G, 1998. Politics in the fine meshes: young citizens, power and media. *Media, Culture & Society*, Vol 20, pp 201–218.

Bentivegna S, 2002. Politics and new media. In Lievrouw L and Livingstone S, eds. *The Handbook of New Media: Social Shaping and Consequences of ICTs*. London: Sage. pp 50–61.

Bhaskar R, 1989. *Reclaiming Reality: A Critical Introduction to Contemporary Philosophy*. London: Verso.

Carpini M X D, 2000. *Gen.com: youth, civic engagement, and the new information environment. Political Communication*. 17 (4), pp 341–349.

Choudrie J and Lee H, 2004. Broadband development in South Korea: institutional and cultural factors. *European Journal of Information Systems*, 13 (2), pp 103–114.

Coleman S, 2004. Connecting Parliament to the Public via the Internet: Two Case Studies of Online Consultations. *Information, Communication & Society*, 7 (1), pp 1–22.

Coleman S, 2005. The network-employed citizen: how people share civic knowledge on line. [Online]. Available from: http://www.ippr.org.uk/uploadedFiles/research/projects/Digital_Society/the_networkempowered_citizen_coleman.pdf [accessed 3 March 2006].

Danermark B, et al, 1997. *Explaining Society: Critical Realism in the Social Sciences*. London and New York: Routledge.

Donga Ilbo (2000). Easing hair style regulations. 4 October. [online] Available from: http://news.naver.com/news/read.php?mode=LSD&office_id=020&article_id=0000029139&section_id=102&menu_id=102 [accessed 5 June 2007].

Donga Ilbo (2005). Demonstration: No cut. 16 May. [online] Available from: http://news.naver.com/news/read.php?mode=LSD&office_id=020&ar

ticle_id=0000299142&section_id=102&menu_id=102 [accessed 5 June 2007].

Friedland L A and Morimoto S, 2006. The lifeworlds of young people and civic engagement. In P. Levine and J. Youniss, ed. *Youth Civic Engagement: An Institutional Turn*. College Park, MD: The Center for Information & Research on Civic Learning & Engagement, 2006, pp 37–39.

Guardian (2003). World's first internet president logs on. 24 Feb. [online] Available from: http://www.guardian.co.uk/korea/article/0,2763,901445,00. html [accessed 5 June 2007].

Hall R and Newbury D, 1999. What makes you switch on? Young people, the Internet and cultural participation. In Sefton-Green J, ed. *Young People, Creativity and New Technologies*. London: Routledge. pp 100–110.

ITU – *see* International Telecommunication Union

International Telecommunication Union, 2007. ICT statistics database. [Online]. Available from: http://www.itu.int/ITU-D/icteye/Indicators/Indicators.aspx# [accessed 5 June 2007].

Katz J E et al, 2001. The Internet, 1995-2000: Access, Civic Involvement, and Social Interaction. *American Behavioral Scientist*, 45 (3), pp 405–419.

Kim H, Moon J and Yang S, 2004. Broadband penetration and participatory politics: South Korea case. *Proceedings of the 37th Hawaii International Conference on Systems Sciences.*

Lee H and Choudrie J, 2002. Investigating broadband technology deployment in South Korea. *Brunel-DTI International Technology Services Mission to South Korea.*

Lee H, O'Keefe R M and Yun K, 2003. The Growth of Broadband and Electronic Commerce in South Korea: Contributing Factors. *The Information Society*, 19 (1), pp 81–93.

Livingstone S and Bober M, 2005. Final report 'UK Children Go Online: Final report of key project findings' (published 28 April 2005), London: London School of Economics and Political Science.

Livingstone S, et al, 2005. Active participation or just more information? Young people's take up of opportunities to act and interact on the Internet. *Information, Communication & Society*, 8 (3), pp 287–314.

National Internet Development Agency of Korea, 2006. [Online]. Available from http://isis.nida.or.kr/index_unssl.jsp [accessed 5 June 2007].

OECD, 2005. OECD Broadband Statistics, June 2005. [Online]. Available from: http://www.oecd.org/document/16/0,3343,en_2649_34223_35526608_1_1_1_1,00.html#Graphs2005. [accessed 5 June 2007]

Prensky M, 2001. Digital Natives, Digital Immigrants. *On the Horizon*, 9 (5), pp 1–6.

Putnam R D, 2000. *Bowling Alone: The Collapse and Revival of American Community*. New York: Simon & Schuster.

Putnam R D, 1995. Bowling Alone: America's Declining Social Capital. *Journal of Democracy*, 6 (1), pp 65–78.

Rice R E and Katz J E, 2004. The Internet and Political Involvement in 1996 and 2000. In Howard, Philip N & Jones S, eds. *Society Online: the Internet in Context*. Thousand Oaks, CA: Sage, 2004.

USTODAY.com (2005) Internet boom alters political process in Iran. 6 December. [Online]. Available from: http://www.usatoday.com/news/world/2005-06-12-iran-election-internet_x.htm [accessed 3 March 2006].

Yonhap News, 2005a. 2008 university entrance, big bang. 17 April. [Online]. Available from: http://news.naver.com/news/read.php?mode=LSD&office_id=001&article_id=0000977429&section_id=100&menu_id=100 [accessed 5 June 2007].

Yonhap News, 2005b. Opposition to the relative assessment of high school grade points. 7 May. Available from: http://news.naver.com/news/read.php?mode=LSD&office_id=001&article_id=0000996294&section_id=102&menu_id=102 [accessed 5 June 2007].

Youniss J, et al, 2002. Youth civic engagement in the twenty-first century. *Journal of Research on Adolescence*, 12 (1), pp 121–148.

6

Generations of care: demographic change and public policy in Australia

Deborah Brennan

Introduction

Demographic changes, particularly declining fertility and the ageing of the population, present significant social and political challenges for Australia even though, in comparison with many European countries, the changes forecast for Australia are not dramatic. There is widespread agreement among Australian policy makers that a higher proportion of the population will need to be engaged in paid work in order to sustain the growing proportion of elderly people that is forecast from mid-century[1].

To date, most attention has focused on measures to retain the skills of older workers and to compel various categories of welfare recipients to engage in paid work. Far less attention has been given to increasing the labour force participation of women who are in neither of these categories, for example those who have only limited attachment to the workforce. This is curious, since Australian women, especially mothers, have relatively low levels of labour force participation compared with their counterparts in comparable countries, and a very high incidence of part-time work. The highly gendered distribution of unpaid work, especially caring responsibilities, is widely acknowledged to be a major reason for women's low levels of labour force participation: women do a disproportionate share of the work of caring for children, the elderly and people with disabilities. This chapter examines the adequacy of some of the key public policies and

---

[1] While a great deal of attention has focused on the 'costs' of an ageing society, any balanced view must take into account the fact that older people contribute in numerous way to their families and communities. On one estimate, men and women aged over 65 contributed more than $39 billion in unpaid work for their families and communities in 1997 (de Vaus et al, 2003).

workplace arrangements that support the balancing of paid work and caring responsibilities. It argues that Australia needs greater levels of government support and more commitment from employers in order to enhance the ability of those with caring responsibilities to engage in paid work and thus meet the challenge of structural ageing.

The first part of the chapter examines the background to the demographic debate in Australia and considers why the relationship between paid work and unpaid care is so important for Australia's future. It introduces the notion of the 'sandwich generation' and shows why policies that support gender equity and work/family balance are important in meeting the demographic challenge. The second part looks at the distribution of paid and unpaid work in Australia and the 'care penalty' faced by many Australian women. The third section offers an analysis of three key work/family policy areas – maternity leave, child care and elder care. The final section summarises the arguments and offers some reflections and conclusions.

Demographic change, work and care

According to the *Intergenerational Report* – the Australian Treasury's first detailed assessment of the consequences of population ageing – the proportion of the Australian population aged 65 or more will double to about 25 per cent by 2040 (Australian Treasury, 2002; Henry, 2003) with consequent effects on the aged 'dependency ratio' (the proportion of the population aged 65 and over to those aged 15–64). Of particular concern is the growth in the numbers of those deemed to be 'very old', that is aged 85 or more. By 2050, the number of Australians in this age group will increase from around 300,000 to 1.4 million or six per cent of the population (Productivity Commission, 2005: 8). Significant health care and pension costs will be associated with this increase in longevity and this has raised concerns about how to increase labour force participation. The Treasury, noting that Australia's labour force participation rate is ranked twelfth amongst the countries of the OECD, has argued that there is 'significant potential to improve participation both in the short and medium term' (Australian Treasury, 2004: 1). One notable aspect of the debate about demography and public policy in Australia has been the reluctance of key policy makers to acknowledge the connection between the distribution of caring responsibilities (both within households and between families and the state) and participation in the labour market. Although the need to increase labour force participation is a constant theme in debates about Australia's social and economic future, there has been limited focus on the measures necessary to make workforce participation sustainable for those with caring responsibilities. Likewise, there has been little recognition, at least in official discourse, of the heavily gendered nature of these effects.

Research conducted for the Business Council of Australia (BCA) has reinforced the Australian Treasury's argument about labour force participation. In a report commissioned by the BCA, *Australia's Population Future*, Glenn Withers has shown that the labour force currently grows by 180,000 per year; in the decade from 2020 it is projected to grow at a mere 14,000 per year (Withers, 2004: 4). Withers compares the labour force participation rates of men and women in Australia, Canada, USA and the UK, identifying 'best practice' (i.e. the highest level of workforce participation) for each age group. He then calculates the number of people who would be added to the Australian labour force if Australia were to achieve 'best practice'. The results are shown in Table 6.1 (below) which identifies over 628,000 'missing workers' (Withers' term), more than three-quarters of whom are women. Remarkably, however, there is little discussion in *Australia's Population Future* of the reasons for Australian women's relatively low labour force participation or the measures that would need to be taken by governments and businesses in order to support higher levels of labour force participation by women.

Table 6.1. Labour force participation change to best practice: Australia

	Australian LFPR 25+ (%)		Best practice LFPR 25+ (%)		Implied added workers	
	Men	Women	Men	Women	Men	Women

25-29	90.1	74.3	92.3	80.5	15,806	44,224
30-34	92.1	67.4	93.8	79.3	12,256	87,052
35-39	91.3	70.2	92.0	79.9	11,827	71,222
40-44	91.1	74.2	92.3	81.6	8574	54,724
45-49	89.3	75.4	91.2	79.7	12,986	29,371
50-54	85	66.3	86.6	74.1	10,601	49,806
55-59	70.7	49.5	77.2	61.7	33,522	60,834
60-64	46.6	21.4	56.6	42.5	40,766	84,553
					146,339	481,786
						628,124

Source: Withers, 2004: 9.

The absence of work/family reconciliation measures is not the only barrier to workforce participation. Other factors such as low levels of education, ill health, employer discrimination and lack of flexibility in employment all play a role. But the lack of support for workers with caring responsibilities is critical. Large numbers of Australians have some level of responsibility for another adult (usually a parent or spouse) or a child; increasing numbers have responsibility for both (Jackson, 2001: 33). The Human Rights and Equal Opportunity Commission (HREOC, 2005) notes that the phenomenon of being 'sandwiched' between the generations results from three changes that have occurred in recent decades: first, babies are being born later in women's lives – the median age of married mothers giving birth for the first time has been rising since 1972 and reached a record high of 30.4 in 2004 (ABS, 2004a). Second, people are living longer and remaining in their own homes as long as possible, rather than moving into residential care (see below); and third, young adult children are living at home for longer (de Vaus, 2004: 144-145; see also Miller, 1981; Nichols & Junk, 1997; Roots, 1998; Ingersoll-Dayton et al, 2001; Raphael & Schlesinger, 2004).

The impact of caring for elderly, ill, or disabled parents, spouses and children has been under-researched in comparison to the need for child care – although studies by Watson and Mears (1989, 1999) on 'women in the middle' provide notable exceptions. Recent important work has begun to redress this imbalance. The *Survey of Disability, Ageing and Carers* published by the Australian Bureau of Statistics (ABS, 2003), for example, showed that 2.6 million Australians provide some assistance to the elderly and people with disabilities. Women comprise just over half of all carers, but represent 71 per cent of primary carers (the ABS defines a primary carer is defined as the one who provides the most informal assistance, in terms of help or supervision, to a person with one or more disabilities which impair core activities of communication, mobility and self-care). Looking at the same phenomenon from a different perspective, the Australian Longitudinal Study on Women's Health data show that 40 per cent of mid-age women provide care for someone who is elderly, frail or ill, and over 40 per cent also provide care, at least occasionally, for children (Warner-Smith et al, 2005).

Paid employment and caring responsibilities

Policies that shape decision-making about the balance between paid work and family care are the subject of intense debate and policy innovation in many countries. In the last three decades, new patterns of family formation and dissolution have arisen, demographic patterns have changed, and new trends in labour market participation have emerged. Across Europe, governments have responded to these challenges by expanding the options available to parents and other carers (Lister, 2002; Ellingsaeter & Leira, 2006; Daly, 2004). Expenditure on child care has grown, parental leave (including special provisions for fathers' leave) has been extended and a variety of measures relating to working time (including the right to move from full-time to part-time work and the ability to choose flexible scheduling) have become part of the policy repertoire in OECD countries. There is also evidence of innovation and policy development in a number of Asian countries (Sung, 2002; Peng, 2002). How are work and care distributed in Australia and how have governments and employers responded to the growing number of carers at work? This section looks first at men's and women's patterns of paid work and unpaid care and then examines three key family benefits: maternity leave, child care and elder care.

Many carers in Australia have paid work in addition to unpaid caring responsibilities, but they are frequently limited to part-time or casual jobs. An Australian survey conducted in 1998 showed that one in four employed primary carers often needed time off work and a small but significant proportion – just under seven per cent – had been obliged to leave work completely within the last three months because of their care responsibilities (ABS, 1998). Another large group had withdrawn from the labour force completely because they were unable to manage both paid work and unpaid care responsibilities (ABS, 1998). The latter scenario is particularly likely to be true of female primary carers. Close to one quarter of all primary carers stated that they had left work prior to taking on a full-time caring role, while 30.7 per cent said they did not have paid work before taking on the caring role (ABS, 1998). Current arrangements did not necessarily reflect the 'choices' of these carers. Of those primary carers not currently employed, about 40 per cent expressed a desire to be employed but were faced with substantial barriers such as difficulty in arranging care, lack of alternative care options and loss of skills from being outside the workforce (ABS, 1998; see also Cass, 2002, 2005).

The postwar years, especially the last three decades, have seen a revolution in women's lives with more and more mothers contributing financially to their families through paid work (Bittman, 2004; Craig, 2005). But there has not been a corresponding revolution in men's lives (Pocock, 2003). Very few men share household chores equitably with their partners, even when both work full-time. The attitudes and practices of most employers have failed to adapt to changes in women's labour force participation and in the aspirations of many men and women about what constitutes a good parent in today's society. The inflexibility of many workplaces results in women being relegated to part-time and casual employment that is well below their skills and capacities. The assumption that the 'ideal worker' puts in long hours and is available to work weekends and evenings, creates problems both for men and women. Research consistently shows that men would like more involvement with their children (Bowman & Russell, 2000), and women would like decent jobs and pay and do not wish to be relegated to poor quality casual employment (Pocock, 2003).

The proportion of Australian women who are employed increased from 40 per cent in 1979 to 53 per cent in 2004; in the same period, men's employment declined from 74 per cent to 68 per cent. Women now represent 45 per cent of the labour force (ABS, 2006b). Looking simply at these aggregate data it appears that men's and women's rates of labour force participation are coming closer together. Once we dig below the surface, however, major differences appear. Participation in paid work falls significantly for women around childbearing age and rises later in life. Many mothers work part-time, especially when their children are young. In 2003, 36 per cent were employed part-time, 25 per cent were employed full-time and just under 40 per cent were outside the labour force (HREOC, 2005: 15; Austen & Giles, 2003). Lone mothers are a little less likely than married mothers to be employed when they have young children, however, changes to the welfare system from the middle of 2006 will compel many sole parents into part-time work. Most Australian fathers work full-time, often for very long hours. Around 33 per cent of fathers work 35-40 hours ('standard' hours), 22 per cent work 41-48 hours, 24 per cent work 49-59 hours and 22 per cent usually work 60 hours or more (Weston et al, 2004: 9). Family friendly benefits such as flexible start and finish times, work-based child care and maternity and parental leave are concentrated in the public sector and amongst better paid, 'high value' employees (Gray & Tudball, 2002).

The presence of children barely makes a dent in men's labour force participation. Most fathers are employed full-time. For mothers, however, the situation is entirely different. More than 60 per cent of mothers of dependent children were employed in 2003, a significant rise from the 46 per cent employed in 1985 (Campbell & Charlesworth, 2004: 77). Compared with women in comparable countries, however, Australian women have a relatively low level of workforce participation. In 2000, only 43 per cent of Australian women with two or more children were in the workforce, compared with 82 per cent in Sweden, 65 per cent in the United States and 62 per cent in the United Kingdom (Campbell & Charlesworth, 2004:

A2-12). The presence of children has a profound impact on women's engagement with the labour market. Participation dips for women around the time of childbirth and childrearing and rises as children grow older. The employment rate for mothers is around 46 per cent when their youngest child is less than five years; it rises to 66 per cent when the youngest child is aged 5–9 years and to 70 per cent when the youngest is 10–14 years (FaCS & AIFS, 2005: 11).

Support for the caring roles of workers

Given the level of official concern about Australia's low level of labour force participation, we might expect that public policies and workplace practices to support working carers would be widespread. In fact, there are significant gaps and anomalies in Australia's approach to the support of workers with caring responsibilities (Pocock, 2003). In this section of the paper, I review three areas of policy that are central to helping workforce participants manage the responsibilities of care – maternity leave, child care and services for the elderly.

Maternity leave

For any government wanting to increase the participation of women in the labour force, paid maternity leave is a logical place to start. There is a clear association between paid maternity leave and women's long-term participation in the labour force (Kamerman, 2000). Unpaid leave does not have the same effect and indeed long periods of unpaid leave can work in the opposite direction – strengthening the idea of the male breadwinner and reinforcing women's dependence. Australia and the USA are the only two OECD countries that do not provide paid maternity leave as a normal workforce provision (HREOC, 2002a: s. 4.1; Baird et al, 2003). Almost all of Australia's major trading partners, including China, Korea, Malaysia, Indonesia, Hong Kong, India, Singapore and Thailand also provide such leave (HREOC, 2002a: ss. 4.3-4.4). In 2002, following a comprehensive public consultation, HREOC proposed a system of government-funded maternity leave that would have provided all new mothers (including the self-employed) with twelve weeks pay at minimum

wages
(HREOC, 2002b). The government rejected this proposal, opting instead for a 'maternity payment' which is unrelated to workforce participation and is worth less than twelve weeks minimum wages.

Despite the absence of a national scheme, approximately 40 per cent of Australian employees are entitled to a period of paid maternity leave through an award, agreement or other workplace provision (Pocock, cited in O'Neill, 2004). There are vast differences in access to this benefit across industries and occupations, as well as significant differences in duration and remuneration. Some 77 per cent of women in the finance and insurance industries have access to paid maternity leave, while only one per cent are covered in the retail sector, and two per cent in hotels and restaurants (O'Neill, 2004). Those most likely to receive the benefit are employed in large, unionised workplaces and/or are considered 'high value' individuals.

A survey on paid maternity leave conducted by the Equal Opportunity for Women in the Workplace Agency (EOWWA) casts further light on the nature and distribution of this benefit. The survey looked at the nature and extent of maternity leave in organisations that report to it under the *Equal Opportunity for Women in the Workplace Act 1999* (Cwlth). The legislation covers higher education institutions and private sector organisations that employ 100 or more employees. Over one million women workers – around a quarter of the female workforce – work for such organisations. Given the nature of the organisations surveyed, and the fact that, by definition, all are subject to equal opportunity legislation, it would be reasonable to expect a relatively high level of paid maternity leave on offer. In fact, the survey found that only 41 per cent of the organisations provided paid maternity leave. While this was an improvement on earlier years (23 per cent provided paid maternity leave in 2001 and 36 per cent in 2003) it is still unacceptably low. Not only that, but the modal duration of paid maternity leave amongst the organisations surveyed was just six weeks; only five per cent of the organisations providing paid leave offered the 14 weeks recommended by the International Labour Organisation and only 37 per cent made the leave available to all female employees, including casuals (EOWWA, 2005: 10). Overall, the absence of a national system of paid maternity leave fundamentally undercuts women's attachment to the labour force. It drives home the notion that there is a penalty associated with combining paid work and care and sends a signal to women that their work is seen as less important than men's work. This is completely at odds with the message delivered by the *Intergenerational Report*.

Child care

Child care is another element of social policy that is vital for the support of workers with family responsibilities, especially given the growth in labour force participation of mothers. Child care has become a major political issue since the 1970s and services have grown rapidly in recent years (Brennan, 1998). About half of all children aged under 12 in Australia use some form of child care (either formal or informal[2]). Importantly for the intergenerational debate, grandparents are significant providers of child care. In 2005, 631,400 children were cared for by their grandparents – more than the combined total of children who attended long day care centres (323,800), family day care homes (106,100) and occasional care (49,500) services (ABS, 2005).[3] Reliance upon the older generation (many of whom are of workforce age, and indeed are workforce participants) to provide child care has significant implications for their willingness and ability to engage more intensively with the labour market.

The Howard government has followed the trail opened up by Labor, encouraging private providers to enter the market, offering cash subsidies to families on a means-tested basis and marginalising the type of community-based, non-profit care for which Australia was once known internationally. As a result of the promotion of market alternatives to community-based provision, Australian child care has become 'big business' and private, for-profit providers dominate the

---

[2] Formal care refers to services that are regulated (e.g. long day care, family day care, outside school hours care). Informal care is not regulated. It is arranged by a child's parent(s) either in the child's home or elsewhere and may be paid or unpaid.

[3] Many children use more than one form of care.

provision of care for children below school age (Brennan 2007). A number of childcare companies have now listed on the stock exchange. The largest of these is ABC Learning, owned by Eddy Groves who, in 2006, had a personal wealth estimated at $260 million and was named the richest person under 40 in Australia. Approximately 70 per cent of long day care services are now owned by
private-for-profit businesses (AIHW, 2005). Other forms of care, which are not so profitable, remain in the hands of non-profit community organisations. Thus, around 96 per cent of outside school hours care, 97 per cent of family day care and 99 per cent of occasional care is provided under such auspices (AIHW, 2005).

The shift to the private sector has resulted in a rapid expansion of long day care places. However, there are indications of downward pressure on standards and quality. As community childcare has declined as a percentage of all Commonwealth services, pressures to reduce licensing standards and to abandon the existing system of accreditation in favour of industry self-regulation have intensified. When state regulations have been reviewed, interventions by private child-care lobby groups have, almost without exception, been directed towards driving standards down. In 2003, ABC Learning challenged the Queensland regulations concerning staffing during lunchtime and breaks (Horin, 2003). Corporate providers are, of course, legally obliged to maximise profits for their shareholders. If regulations governing staff qualifications, group sizes, adult/child ratios and basic health, nutrition and safety requirements are seen as barriers to profit, then at least from a business perspective it may be quite appropriate to try to reduce such ‘costs’ (Teghtsoonian, 1993).

Recent research conducted by the Australia Institute has raised concern about the quality of care being provided in childcare centres that are part of corporate chains. Independent private centres offer a level of care that is similar to community based, non-profit centres. On the critical issue of staff members’ own perceptions of their ability to form relationships with children, community-based and independent centres performed significantly better than the corporate chains, with about half the staff from the former two types of care agreeing that they always have time to develop individual relationships, compared to only a quarter at corporate centres (Rush, 2006).

One of the major issues in the provision of early childhood services is the lack of detailed, consultative planning. Macro level data are available from the Australian Bureau of Statistics, but local level planning is noticeably absent. Rudimentary data are available in respect of outside school hours care, family day care and in-home care, since existing services are asked to record the number of places requested. The Department of Family and Community Services and Indigenous Affairs does not, however, measure unmet demand for long day. Thus, the one service type in respect of which *no planning* occurs is long day care – the service which accounts for the largest share of the child care budget and the biggest number of childcare places. With respect to long day care, the market literally rules. Private providers can establish services wherever they wish and, so long as those services become part of the Quality Improvement and Accreditation System, users of these services will be eligible for Child Care Benefit.

The cost of childcare to parents is a highly sensitive issue in Australia. The Australian Government provides Child Care Benefit (CCB) to reduce the costs that parents face in using approved[4] care. Up to fifty hours of CCB is payable if parent(s) meet a work test, and 24 hours CCB is available to other families. The amount of CCB depends upon various factors including family income, the ages of children in care and the number of hours of care required. At the extreme, a family with an income below $34,300 (including those on income support) may be eligible for up to $148 per week. The CCB tapers down to about $25 per week for the 10 per cent or so of families with

---

[4] 'Approved care' refers to services approved by the Australian Government to receive CCB on behalf of families. Such services can include long day care, family day care, in homecare, outside school hours care and occasional care services. Families can also claim the minimum rate of CCB if their child is attends 'registered care'. This can be care provided by grandparents, relatives and friends – so long as they have registered with the Family Assistance Office.

combined incomes over $98,000. Thus, $148 is the maximum CCB available to a low-income family and $25 is the maximum for a high income family. However, these levels of subsidy are payable only in respect of children below school age who attend the service for 50 hours per week. In 2005, the median number of hours spent in formal care was 10 (down from 11 in 2002) and less than three per cent of children were in long day care for 50 or more hours per week. The proportion of children from low-income families who attend childcare for 50 hours and thus attract the maximum subsidy is likely to be miniscule – particularly since families must pay the difference between CCB and the actual fee charged by the service.

During the 2004 election campaign, the government announced an additional measure, the Child Care Tax Rebate (CCTR) to assist working parents with their childcare costs. CCTR was presented as a 30 per cent rebate on out-of-pocket childcare costs (that is, childcare costs minus Child Care Tax Benefit). After the election, the Treasurer announced that a cap of $4000 would be applied and that the CCTR would not be claimable until 2006. In other words, parents would have to wait for up to two years to claim this benefit. The administrative and record-keeping requirements of the CCTR are complex. The CCTR is based on completely different principles to CCB: it is designed to provide the highest benefits to those with high childcare costs – and, since high childcare costs are strongly correlated with high incomes, it is clear which families will benefit the most. Further, the CCTR is *only* available to offset tax, so low-income families will miss out if the amount for which they are eligible is greater than their tax bill. Partnered women can transfer any unused portion of the rebate to their partners; single mothers have no such option. The CCTR has been criticised from many quarters; it seems plain that it is not intended to address the problem of childcare affordability for those most in need, rather it is a response to intense lobbying from those who represent families in the highest income bracket.

Care of the elderly and people with disabilities

As discussed in Chapter 8, since the early 1980s, Australian policy and provision towards the elderly and disabled has shifted from an emphasis on group facilities such as nursing homes and hostels towards support and care services that enable people to remain within their communities, ideally within their own homes, for as long as possible. Policy towards the elderly emphasises healthy ageing, 'ageing in place' (that is, minimising the likelihood that individuals will have to move from one residence to another as they grow older) and supporting people to live in the community, rather than in government-funded aged care accommodation. These policies have been highly successful. Most older Australians are independent, active members of the community. They provide a great deal of care and support to others – especially spouses, children and grandchildren – and make significant contributions to the community through volunteer work (de Vaus et al, 2004). When they require support for themselves, it is most often provided by family members, especially spouses, daughters and daughters-in-law.

The establishment of the Home and Community Care program (HACC) in 1985 signified a decreased emphasis on residential care services and a new emphasis on community care. HACC provides services to older people as well as to people of all ages with disabilities, and their carers. The program is jointly funded by the Commonwealth and the State/Territory governments, and its purpose is to "avoid premature or inappropriate admission to long-term residential care" (AIHW, 2003: 300). In more recent years it has been supplemented by a range of other policies including Community Aged Care Packages (CACPs), Extended Aged Care at Home (EACH) Packages, Veterans' Home Care, and assistance provided by Day Therapy Centres (DTCs). All these are aimed at supporting aged people to remain living in the community and, in this respect, have been highly successful. Since 1986, there has been a substantial decline in the proportion of elderly people living in institutional care. For some, including those in the oldest age groups, the declines have been very significant. For example, close to half (46 per cent) of women aged 85 or more were living in institutional care in 1986; this had fallen to around one-third (34 per cent) by 2001 (AIHW, 2003: 283). These trends are illustrated in Table 6.2.

Table 6.2. Percentage of people living in institutions, by age, 1986–2001

	65–69	70–74	75–79	80–84	85+
Male					
1986	4.1	5.0	8.7	15.1	29.6
1996	4.0	5.1	7.2	12.2	26.6
2001	3.2	3.3	3.3	9.9	22.7
Female					
1986	3.6	5.7	11.2	23.1	46.1
1996	3.2	4.6	8.3	17.7	41.3
2001	2.6	3.5	7.1	14.9	34.2

Source: de Vaus 2004: 253.

The reduced reliance of older citizens on residential care services has many benefits, however the anticipated growth in the numbers of such people in the community will place significant pressure on families and households to provide additional care and support. In 1998 the ABS estimated that 46 per cent of all older people needed some assistance with the tasks of daily living including transport, mobility, housework, property maintenance, and personal care. The projected increase in the proportion of those aged 85 will have particular ramifications. Across the board, people in this age group have much higher needs for assistance than those aged between 65 and 74. Over 90 per cent of people aged 85 or more are likely to need some assistance, compared with 32 per cent of the 65–74s (ABS, 1998). Partners and children were the most likely to provide these forms of assistance, sometimes but not always as a supplement to formal care services. In 1998, 347,000 people over 65 were living at home and using only informal, unpaid services, while 507,000 were living at home and using formal, paid care. Almost three-quarters of the latter group were also assisted by unpaid carers (AIHW, 2006: 154). Five years later, in 2003, the number of older people at home with only unpaid assistance remained about the same (345,000) despite population growth, while the number using formal care had grown to over 607,000. This suggests that the informal care provided largely by family members is growing rapidly and, while this may have a number of benefits for both carers and those who are cared for, very little attention paid to the labour force prospects of unpaid carers.

As discussed earlier, providing care to another person has a substantial impact upon the prospects of the carer finding and maintaining paid work. This has consequences not only for individuals but also for particular occupations and industries, depending upon their age and gender profile. The typical nurse, for example, is a woman in her mid-40s. Many such women are looking after elderly parents as well as young children. The NSW Nurses Association has already identified the absence of elder care facilities as a problem for recruitment and retention in their industry.

As noted above, the impact of child care responsibilities on labour force participation has attracted considerable attention in Australia, far more than the impact of caring for elderly, sick and disabled family members. Yet providing care for this latter group is likely to be a critical issue in years to come, leading to a greater demand for paid carers but also increasing the pressures on family members (mainly women) who assume responsibility for providing informal assistance. While the proportion of those caring for children may fall, there will be a substantial increase in the number of elderly people and also people with disabilities and consequently an increase in need for care for these groups. According to some observers, Australia is already facing a critical shortage of aged care facilities. Pru Warrilow, director of a work/life balance advisory service in Sydney argues that 'the shortage of good aged care facilities is almost as bad as the shortage of care for 0–2 year old children' (quoted in ABC Online, 2003).

Unlike child care, where there are recognisable milestones and a reasonable assumption that the period of greatest dependency will last 3-5 years, no such assumptions can be made about care for the elderly. In addition, the nature of the responsibilities can be unpredictable and the length of time for which care is required is almost always uncertain. Much of this care is, of course, provided very gladly and the argument here is not that family carers should abandon their posts and undertake paid work – or more paid work than they already do. Rather, the argument is that government policy needs to look carefully at the social impacts of the growing need for care in the community, and put more emphasis on enabling carers to combine paid work and care, should they choose to do so, in the least stressful ways possible.

Conclusion

Increasing labour force participation in Australia is widely seen as necessary to compensate for the reduction in the proportion of the population that will be of workforce age in the future, as well as to provide the tax base necessary to meet the income support, health and other needs of an ageing population. A high proportion of the adult population (particularly women) already bears significant responsibility for others, both younger and older, and this proportion is likely to rise with the increased longevity of the population and the increasing incidence of disability in the population. Measures to support the workforce engagement of those with caring responsibilities will be vital in coming decades. This chapter has reviewed three areas of public provision for workers with family responsibilities – maternity leave, child care and support services for the elderly. In each of these there is considerable scope for more creative policy thinking as well as more substantial public investment in order to support both carers and those in receipt of care.

References

ABC (Australian Broadcasting Corporation) Online, 2003. *The World Today – Nurses Push for Elderly Daycare* [online]. Available from: http://www.abc.net.au/worldtoday/content/ 2003/s912780.htm [accessed 8 November 2006].

ABS – *see* Australian Bureau of Statistics.

Australian Bureau of Statistics, 2005. *Childcare*, Cat. No. 4402.0

Australian Bureau of Statistics, 1998. *Survey of Disability, Ageing and Carers*, Cat. No. 4430.0.

Australian Bureau of Statistics. 2003. *Survey of Disability, Ageing and Carers*, Cat. No. 4430.0

Australian Bureau of Statistics, 2004a. *Births*, Cat. No. 3301.0.

Australian Bureau of Statistics, 2004b. *Disability, Ageing and Carers: Summary of findings* 2004 Cat. No. 4430.0.

Australian Bureau of Statistics, 2006a. *Barriers and Incentive to Labour Force Participation, Australia, Aug 2004 to Jun 2005*, Cat. No. 6239.0, February.

Australian Bureau of Statistics, 2006b. *Australian Social Trends*, Cat. No. 4102.0, July 2006.

AIHW – *see* Australian Institute of Health and Welfare

Australian Institute of Health and Welfare, 2003. *Australia's Welfare*. AIHW.

Australian Institute of Health and Welfare, 2006. *Australia's Welfare*. AIHW.

EOWA – *see* Equal Opportunity for Women in the Workplace Agency .

Equal Opportunity for Women in the Workplace Agency, 2005. *Equal Opportunity for Women in the Workplace Survey, Paid Maternity Leave* [online]. Available from: http://www.eowa.gov.au/ [accessed 8 November 2006].

Australian Treasury, 2002. *Intergenerational Report*, Budget Paper No. 5. Canberra: Commonwealth of Australia.

Australian Treasury, 2004. *Australia's Demographic Challenges*, Canberra: Commonwealth of Australia.

Austen S. and Giles M, 2003. The Likely Effects of Ageing on Women's Involvement in the Paid Workforce. *Australian Bulletin of Labour*, 29 (3), pp 253–273.

Baird M, Brennan D and Cutcher L, 2002. A Pregnant Pause in the Provision of Paid Maternity Leave in Australia. *Labour and Industry*, 12 (4)

Banks G, 2004. An ageing Australia: small beer or big bucks? *Address to the South Australian Centre for Economic Studies* [online]. Available from: http://www.pc.gov.au/speeches/cs20040429/index.html [accessed 8 November 2006].

Bittman M, 2004. Parenting and Employment: What time-use surveys show. In Folbre N and Bittman M, eds *Family Time: The social organization of care*. London: Routledge.

Bowman L and Russell G, 2000. *Work and Family: Current thinking, research and practice*. Sydney: Macquarie Research.

Brennan D, 2007. The ABC of Child Care Politics. *Australian Journal of Social Issues*, 14 (2) pp 213-225.

Brennan D, 1998. *The Politics of Australian Childcare: Philanthropy, Feminism and Beyond*. Cambridge: Cambridge University Press.

Campbell I and Charlesworth S, 2004. *Key Work and Family Trends in Australia.* Melbourne: Centre for Applied Social Research, RMIT.

Cass B, 2002. Employment Time and Family Time: The Intersections of Labour Market Transformations and Family Responsibilities in Australia. In Callus R and Lansbury R, eds *Working Futures: The Changing Nature of Work and Employment Relations in Australia.* Sydney: Federation Press, pp 142–167.

Cass B, 2005. Women as Carers: Economic and Social Aspects of Caring. Paper presented at Women, Ageing and Participation Workshop, Brisbane.

Craig L, 2005. The Money or the Care? A comparison of couple and sole parent households' time allocation to work and children. Australian Journal of Social Issues, 40 (4), pp 521–540.

Daly M, 2004. Changing Conceptions of Family and Gender Relations in European Welfare States and the Third Way. In Lewis J and Surender R, eds *Welfare State Change: Towards a Third Way?* Oxford: Oxford University Press.

de Vaus D, 2004. *Diversity and Change in Australian Families: Statistical Profiles*. Melbourne: Australian Institute of Family Studies.

de Vaus D, Gray M and Stanton D, 2004. The Value of Unpaid Work of Older Australians. *Family Matters*, 66 (Spring/Summer, 34–39).

Ellingsaeter, A. L. and Leira, A., 2006. *Politicising Parenthood in Scandinavia: Gender Relations in Welfare States*. Bristol: The Policy Press.

EOWWA – *see* Equal Opportunity for Women in the Workplace Agency

Equal Opportunity for Women in the Workplace Agency (EOWWA), 2005. Equal Opportunity for Women in the Workplace Survey 2004. Paid Maternity Leave. EOWWA, Sydney.

FaCS and AIFS ([Department of] Family and Community Services and Australian Institute of Family Studies, 2005. *Growing Up in Australia: The longitudinal study of Australian Children – Annual Report 2004*. Melbourne: Commonwealth of Australia.

Fine M, 1999. *The Responsibility for Child and Aged Care: Shaping Policies for the Future*, August 1999, SPRC Discussion Paper No. 105.

Gray M and Tudball J, 2002. Access to Family Friendly Work Practices: Differences within and between Australian workplaces. *Family Matters*, 61, pp 30–55.

Henry K, 2003. Economic Prospects and Policy Challenges. *Address to the Australian Business Economists*. Sydney, 20 May 2003. Available from: http://www.treasury.gov.au/documents /639/HTML/docshell.asp?URL=speach_%20main.asp [accessed 12 August 2006].

Horin A, 2003. When Making Money is Child's Play. *Sydney Morning Herald*, 4 October.

HREOC – *see* Human Rights and Equal Opportunity Commission.

Human Rights and Equal Opportunity Commission, 2002a. *Valuing Parenthood: Options for Paid Maternity Leave*. Interim Paper [online]. Sydney: HREOC. Available from: http://www.hreoc.gov.au/sex_discrimination/pml/index.html [accessed 26 November 2006].

Human Rights and Equal Opportunity Commission, 2002b. *A Time to Value: Proposal for a National Paid Maternity Leave Scheme* [online]. Sydney: HREOC. Available from: http://www.hreoc.gov.au/sex_discrimination/pml2/index.html [accessed 26 November 2006].

Human Rights and Equal Opportunity Commission, 2005. *Striking the Balance: Women, Men, Work and Family* [online]. Sydney: HREOC. Available from: http://www.hreoc.gov.au/sex_discrimination/strikingbalance/index.html [accessed 26 November 2006].

Ingersoll-Dayton B, Neal M B and Hammer L B, 2001. Aging parents helping adult children: The experience of the sandwiched generation. *Family Relations: Interdisciplinary Journal of Applied Studies*, 50, pp 262–271.

Jackson N, 2001. *The Policy-Maker's Guide to Population Ageing: Key concepts and issues* Policy Research Paper No 13 Department of Family and Community Services, Canberra.

Kamerman S, 2000. Parental Leave Policies: An Essential Ingredient in Early Childhood Education and Care Policies. *Social Policy Report*, 14 (2), pp 3–15.

Lister R, 2002. The Dilemmas of Pendulum Politics: Balancing Paid Work, Care and Citizenship *Economy and Society*, 31, pp 520–32.

Miller D, 1981. The 'sandwich' generation: Adult children of the aging. *Social Work*, 26, pp 419–423.

Nichols L S, and Junk V W, 1997. The sandwich generation: Dependency, proximity, and task assistance needs of parents. *Journal of Family and Economic Issues*, 18, pp 299–326.

O'Neill S, 2004. *Paid Maternity Leave*, E-Brief: Online Only, Issued 13 September 2002; updated 11 August 2004. Available from: http://www.aph.gov.au/library/intguide/ECON/ maternity_leave.htm [accessed 7 March 2006].

Peng I, 2002. Gender and Generation: Japanese Childcare and the Demographic Crisis. In Michel S and Mahon R, eds *Childcare Policy at the Crossroads: Gender and Welfare State Restructuring*. New York: Routledge.

Pocock B, 2003. *The Work/Life Collision*. Sydney: Federation Press.

Productivity Commission, 2005. *Economic Implications of an Ageing Australia, Overview* [online]. Available from: http://www.pc.gov.au [accessed 26 November 2006].

Raphael D and Schlesinger B, 1994. Women in the sandwich generation: Do adult children living at home help? *Journal of Women & Aging*, 6, pp 21–45.

Roots C R, 1998. *The sandwich generation: Adult children caring for aging parents*. New York: Garland Publishing.

Rush E, 2006. *Childcare Quality in Australia*. Canberra: Australia Institute.

Sung S, 2002. Women Reconciling Paid and Unpaid Work in a Confucian Welfare State: The Case of South Korea. *Social Policy and Administration*, 37 (4), pp 342–360.

Teghtsoonian K, 1993. Neo-conservative Ideology and Opposition to Federal Regulation of Childcare Services in the United States and Canada. *Canadian Journal of Political Science*, 26, pp 97–121.

Warner-Smith P, Everingham C and Ford J, 2006. Mid-Age Women's Experiences of Work and Expectations of Retirement. *Just Policy*, 40 (June)

Watson E and Mears J, 1989. *Women in the Middle: Care Givers with a Double Burden of Care*. Macarthur, Sydney: University of Western Sydney.

Watson E and Mears J, 1999. *Women, Work and Care of the Elderly*. Aldershot: Ashgate.

Weston R, Gray M, Qu L and Stanton D, 2004. *Long work hours and the wellbeing of fathers and their families*. AIFS Research paper no. 35. Melbourne: Australian Institute of Family Studies.

Withers G, 2004. *Australia's Population Future: A Position Paper*. Sydney: BCA.

7

Child care support programs for double income families in Korea

Kim Jeong-hee

Introduction

The birth rate in Korea in 2005 was 1.08 children per woman, the lowest in the world. This is a clear indication of the prevailing trend in Korea of 'a family without a child', and mirrors the burdens and difficulties of child care. It is particularly applicable to women in the paid workforce with children: since the gendered division of labour remains solid, these women face double responsibilities, at work and home.

In March 2005, 52.3 per cent of the working population of Korea were full time employees working under contract for a period of over one year; 33.3 per cent were temporary workers who were hired for periods between one month and one year; and 13.4 per cent were daily workers, reflecting overall low levels of job security (KNSO, 2005). Despite the low levels of job security, the increased burden of bringing up children is forcing a growing number of Korean households to become double income families.

This chapter reviews the status of child care arrangements in Korea and the difficulties faced by women in the paid workforce with children. It also puts forward suggestions as to how to address some of these difficulties. Government policies at the national level that support child care for double income families are comprehensive in nature and are also linked to tax exemption, education and other policies.

Although it is acknowledged that bringing up children requires broad social and national support, this chapter focuses specifically on maternity leave, parental leave, childcare services and family participation in child care. It is based on an analysis of literature concerning women in the paid workforce and their use of and access to child care in Korea; in particular, it draws on the national survey on child care conducted by Seo Mun-hee et al (2005) through the sponsorship of the Ministry of Gender Equality and Families and further material from related ministries on women's issues (Seo Mun-hee et al, 2005).

Maternity leave and parental leave

Since liberation from Japanese rule in 1945 and up until recently, maternity leave was the equivalent of 60 days of unpaid leave. 'Protection of motherhood' was the most important issue for the women's movement in Korea in the 1990s and, as a result, three national government bills relating to motherhood protection passed in July 2001. Ninety days *paid* maternity leave became the standard in November 2001. The costs associated with the additional 30 days were funded through employment insurance and the national budget.

As shown in Table 7.1 (below), the percentage of working women who had a child and were given paid maternity leave was 25.1 in 2003 and 31.2 in 2004. In other words, only two to three out of ten women in the paid workforce who gave birth received paid maternity leave.

Since November 2001, when the Motherhood Protection Laws were revised in Korea, any male or female worker with a child under one year of age could take paid parental leave and was entitled to receive W200,000 (equivalent of US $200) per month for 10.5 months in addition to 90 days paid maternity leave. From 2003, the monthly allowance for parental leave was increased to W400,000 (US $400) but still fell short of the minimum monthly wage of W567,260. Table 7.1 (following) shows that only an estimated 25.1 per cent of all women workers in 2003 and 31.2 per cent in 2004 took maternity leave after they gave birth. Such a low rate can be attributed to the fact that maternity leave was granted only to employment insurance beneficiaries.

Table 7.1. Statistics of maternity & parental leave of women workers (2003, 2004) unit: persons, %

Numbers	2003	2004
Newborns (a)	493,471	476,052
Women workers who gave birth (estimates)(b)*	127,809	123,297
Women workers who took maternity leave(c)	32,133	38,541
Women workers who took the parental leave (d)	6816	9303
Rate of maternity leave among women workers(c/b x 100)	25.1	31.2
Rate of parental leave among women workers (c/d x 100)	5.3	7.5

Source: Korea National Statistical Office, 2003. (2004a)

(* b= (a)x 25.9(%))[1]

As at the end of 2004, more that 9.5 million women were economically active. However, the number of women insured was only 1.5 million, or 16 per cent of the economically active female population (Ministry of Labour, 2004; KNSO, 2004c). As stated above, maternity leave is granted only to employment insurance beneficiaries, and 61.3 per cent of women workers as of December 2005 were temporary workers with employment contracts for less than one year (KNSO, 2005). Therefore, the institutionalisation of maternity leave has little impact on the lives of most working mothers.

Table 7.1 also shows that 5.3 per cent of women in the paid workforce in 2003 and 7.5 per cent in 2004 were assumed to have taken *parental* leave, which is much lower than the take up of *maternity* leave. The first possible reason for this is that parental leave, like maternity leave, is granted only to employment insurance beneficiaries. The second reason is that resignation due to childbirth is still dominant in Korea's entrepreneurial culture. As explained by the woman in the example quoted below, as long as parental leave is not made compulsory as it is for national defence commitments, it is unlikely to be practised effectively:

> I am working for a finance company that has relatively good welfare programs, however, thus far only one person has taken parental leave. Everyone said she was very bold. Not to mention how unprecedented it was to take paid leave, everyone wonders if she would be allowed to come back to work after the one-year leave. I am pregnant. I

[1] According to Hwang Su-kyong's analysis of the 5th Korea Labour Panel (2002) survey data, 54.5% of married women, from newly married to before first childbirth, hold jobs. But during the peak of their child care period, which is usually after the first childbirth until the youngest child becomes two years old, only 25.9% of women held jobs (2004: 111–12). 4411 women were selected for the sample analysis. Supposing the sample analysis represents a general picture, 25.9% is believed to be the rate of women working after they gave birth.

> should be happy about it but concerns outweigh the joy, when it is not certain if my desk would still be there even after the 90 day maternity leave. How can I be audacious enough to think about one year's paid parental leave? Unless the leave is made compulsory like the duty for national defence and liability to tax, no one could take the leave with any peace of mind. (Ministry of Labour, homepage, id 'moron') ("I am scared that I would hear 'why don't you take the parental leave?" hani.co.kr 6 Oct 2002)

According to the Ministry of Gender Equality and Family, 39.4 per cent of Korean women gave up their jobs after marriage and 12.6 per cent of them said they quit because of disadvantages at work over pregnancy and childbirth (Seo Mun-hee et al, 2005: 92–93).

In 2004 the parental leave rate increased by only two per cent over the previous year (Table 7.1). Accordingly, in 2005, the government sought various means to make parental leave for child care a viable option. Proposals included: relaxing the requirement for subsidy payment for replacement personnel and increasing the unit price of the subsidy for parental leave; implementing guidance and supervision of the parental leave system for child care; in the case of civil servants, increasing the parental leave period from the current three years to five years, (while at the same time raising the eligible child age from three years to five for mothers to apply for parental leave); and initiating active programs to encourage paternal leave (Joint Response by related Ministries and Organisations, 2005). However, positive results cannot be expected if these proposals are not supported by concrete measures.

In order for the proposal to relax requirements for subsidy payments for replacement personnel and to increase the unit price of the subsidy for parental leave to work effectively, the employer has to be able to replace the worker on leave at more or less an equal level of productivity (in terms of skills and professional qualities). When such conditions are met, the prospective mother can take parental leave without having to worry that her absence would create an extra burden for her co-workers. In March 2005, the Civil Service Commission, a government agency, established a new allowance system for paying 30,000-50,000 *won* per month to co-workers who take on extra work for those who take parental leave (Collecting opinions on running a bank for replacement manpower, 2005). It is highly questionable whether such an allowance, which amounts only to one or two per cent of the monthly salary of the employee taking leave, could effectively replace that employee. Similar problems exist with the 200,000 *won* the government pays to private companies for the leave subsidy and 100,000–150,000 *won* as a replacement subsidy.

As for the guidance and supervision plans to implement the parental leave system and the publicity plans for paternity leave, one could expect positive effects if they are implemented in parallel with subsidy programs that guarantee to meet real costs of living. If the cost of living condition is met, then the guidance and supervision and publicity programs would contribute to creating a child care-friendly culture in companies. It would also give assurance to workers that when they are ready to return to work, their job will still be there.

Further, in order to overcome the limitations of maternity and parental leave, of which the benefits are limited to those receiving employment insurance, a family allowance system should be introduced. Family allowance should apply to every child, and the payment level should be realistic enough to actually alleviate the cost burden of child care. Ways to support direct and indirect costs for women who choose to stay at home to raise children should also be considered (Lee Jae-gyeong et al, 2005). Finland, for example, began building family support systems in 1948, including the introduction of a child allowance system. Child allowance alone reached four per cent of GDP by the 1950s in Finland, and the figure has been increasing continuously since then (Park Hyon-sok, 2005).

Strong regulations at both national and international levels are also required in order to bring about changes to the practice of forcing women to quit jobs after childbirth. A female workers quota system, or the introduction of tax disincentives for enterprises with low maternity leave rates, could be part of a set of national measures. International regulations could also be considered, including regulations banning resignation due to childbirth in international agreements such as the International Standard of Corporate Social Responsibility

(ISCSR). The International Organization for Standardization (ISO) is planning to finalise a draft of the International Standard of Corporate Social Responsibility to come into force by 2008. While international agreements are not binding, non-adherence to them would place an employer organisation at a disadvantage in the international context. Women activists should therefore be forming international alliances to take advantage of such agreements.

Problems with childcare services

A survey conducted by the Ministry of Gender Equality and Families found a clear set of priorities regarding childcare support policies for preschool children. Support for such initiatives emerged in the following order of priority: subsidies (44.7 per cent), diversity of services (18.2 per cent), expansion of public day care centres (17.8 per cent), enforcement and expansion of parental leave (8.7 per cent), better qualified teachers (5.9 per cent), better quality service (3.5 per cent), and improved childcare information (1.1 per cent) (Seo Mun-hee et al, 2005: 387).

As of 2005, only 42.8 per cent of working mothers, 20.1 per cent of unemployed mothers, and 37 per cent of single fathers (or families without a mother) sent their children to day care centres, as reflected in Table 7.2 (below). Further, 40.9 per cent of working mothers sent their children to other educational institutions. Alternately, 44.5 per cent of working mothers' children were placed in the care of blood relatives, 4.7 per cent in the care of parents-in-law, and 27.6 per cent received private tutoring. It was also found that there is a general practice for the parents of children in day care centres to make use of other services as well.

Table 7.2. Status of child care[1] (unit: %, persons)

Division	Infants and kids		
	Working mothers	Non-working mothers	Children without mother
Organisations/childcare givers	71.1	48.9	77.4
Day care centres	42.8	20.1	37.0
Other childcare service organisation (kindergarten, church kindergarten, half day institute, other institutes, study room, and others)	40.9	31.6	52.6
Relatives by blood(residing/non-residing grandparents or relatives)	44.5	6.9	79.6
Relatives–in-law (baby sitters, neighbourhood baby sitters, part-time house keepers)	4.7	0.2	3.7
Private tutoring (home visit tutoring, group tutoring, daily tutor paper)	27.6	31.2	11.3
	(984)	(1917)	(53)

Note 1: figures represent duplicate answers.
(Source: Seo Mun-hee et al (2005) (simplified of the Table 3-3-17) p 117)

In summary, problems with childcare services in Korea are to do with the lack of availability of places, the level of program quality of day care centres, and the affordability of childcare fees.

Availability of places at day care centres

In Korea working hours are long, and so for parents the distance between their home and a childcare facility presents another obstacle to child care. This issue emerged in parents' responses to a survey question that asked: "What is the most important reason for choosing a childcare/child education facility?" In the case of day care centres,

25.6 per cent nominated the distance between home and the facility as the most important reason; in the case of preschools, this was the most important reason for 18.1 per cent of respondents.

> Most pre-school programs provide transport, so the distance can take a backseat to educational programs. In the case of day care centres, it is the parents who need to take the children to the facility so the distance is more important to the working parents who have to go to work after dropping the children at the facility. (Seo Mun-hee et al, 2005: 152).

About half the Korean population lives in apartment buildings, and almost every large apartment complex has an 'elderly pavilion' (a facility for the elderly) next to the children's playground; however, there are only a few day care centres for children in the apartment complexes. Every morning, in energy-scarce Korea, children are shuffled in a van from one neighbourhood to another. Nationwide, the number of day care centres within apartment complexes makes up around 2.8 per cent of the total 670 centres (Joint Response by related Ministries and Organisations, 2005: 31–32). In 2005 the government reviewed the possibility for making childcare facilities[2] mandatory in large apartment complexes, however, the realisation of such a policy is still an open question.

A further problem is that there are insufficient caring hours available at existing centres thus affecting availability of appropriate places. Koreans work longer hours compared with other countries in the world. In 2004, for example, the average annual working hours per person in employment was 1357 hours in the Netherlands, 1363 in Norway, 1585 in Sweden, 1669 in the UK, 1808 in the US and 1816 in Australia. In Korea, it was 2394 hours, making it the highest amongst OECD member countries (OECD, 2006: 265). Working mothers were the subject of a Ministry of Gender Equality and Families survey in 2004 which found that they were working an average 8.4 hours a day (standard deviation 2.5 hours), 48.4 hours a

---

[2] Child care facilities include day care centres, pre-schools and other facilities for child care.

week (standard deviation 18.2 hours) (Seo Mun-hee et al, 2005: 444). Taking the standard deviation into consideration, this equates to 5.9 to 10.9 hours a day, and 36.2 to 60.6 hours a week. This implies that there are working mothers who work longer than 10 hours a day. Considering the daily commuting time, approximately one hour each way, a 12- to 13-hour a day nursery care service is required for double income families.

Table 7.3 (below) clearly shows the need for night time childcare services. A study done by Kim Jeong-hee and others (2004) found that mothers working as nurses, railway station workers, factory workers, journalists, social welfare specialists, bankers, public servants and others, need extra care service beyond that of regular day nurseries (whose standard hours are 7:30 am to 7:30 pm) at least twice a week, either so that they can work overtime or for other job-related activities. The breakdown of the survey data on additional needs was as follows: extra hours service, 27.9 per cent; 24-hour care, 25.8 per cent; and night-time care, 18.4 per cent.

Table 7.3. Night care needs for preschool children (unit: %, persons)

division	yes				No.	total	No. of children
구분	always	1–2 times a week	1–2 times a month	1–2 times a year	58.7	100.0	(2962)
	10.1~14.0	11.8~13.2	10.6~17.7	2.3~4.0	58.7	100.0	(358)

(Source: Seo Mun-hee et al, 2005. (Simplified of the Additional-Table 4-75) p 482).

There is a risk, however, that further availability of night-time child care in day care centres, will reinforce the culture of long working hours for both parents, which in turn would further decrease the potential birth rate if fathers' participation in child care is not increased. While the immediate need for night time care in day care centres should not be ignored, it is more desirable to have fathers' participation in child care increased and overall working hours reduced.

Program quality and affordability in day care centres

The shortage of day care centres does not appear to be the only reason why only 42.8 per cent of working mothers (as shown in Table 7.2) send their children to day care centres. It appears also to relate to the lack of quality services at the centres. Survey results indicate that 36 per cent of working mothers either do not want to send their children to day care centres or were undecided. Of non-working mothers, 23 per cent stated that they would prefer to have a job but felt there was no service to which they could entrust their children (Seo Mun-he et al, 2005: 230, 295).

High quality care and education are composed of various aspects, however, in Korea, the teacher is considered as most important. According to Lee Mihwa et al (2005: 110), 25.7 per cent of nursery school teachers were paid under 790,000 *won* (US$790) monthly; 27.7 per cent were paid 800,000–999,000 *won*; 22.7 per cent were paid 1-1.19 million *won*; 17.1 per cent were paid 1.2–1.39 million *won*; and 6.8 per cent were paid more than 1.4 million *won*. Compared to the average monthly wage of Korean workers, which is 1.750,421 *won*, nursery school teaching is a low paying job (Ministry of Labour, 2005). Such poor working conditions are directly linked to very limited work experience in the field. In 2004, teachers with less than one year's work experience accounted for the highest percentage (32.2 per cent) of those employed in the field; those with 1–2 years' experience made up 21.6 per cent; and those with 2–3 years' experience, 18.4 per cent. Therefore, teachers with less than three years' experience constituted 72.2 per cent of working nursery teachers (Lee Mihwa et al, 2005: 108). This highlights the fact that due to poor conditions it is unlikely that childcare workers will be highly trained professionals with long-term work experience.

In Korean society, teaching at a day care centre is considered a '3D' (difficult, dirty, dangerous) occupation with low wages and poor working conditions. Day care centre teachers are mostly high school graduates who have completed only a one-year course at 'nursing teacher' training centres, rather than a four-year college education majoring in early childhood development or kindergarten education, a further factor in the lack of quality care or education in child care.

Despite dissatisfaction with the quality of child care, there has been no policy response from the government apart from the introduction in 2005 of a childcare facilities certification program. The government's intention in introducing this system was to induce childcare facilities to provide high quality services. However, no specific compensation plans were made for certified childcare facilities. More recently, a discussion has begun on developing a standard childcare procedure. This standard procedure, which is still in the development stage at the Ministry of Gender Equality and Family, distinguishes six areas of development and life activities for children: social relations, communication, physical development, artistic experience, and exploration of natural science (Kim Jeong-won & Kim Il-ok, 2005). A key concern of bio-feminism (the Korean version of eco-feminism) is that children should grow up healthy in body and mind (Kim Jeong-hee, 1998, 2005a,b,c). From this perspective, it is of great concern that current standard procedures do not specify outdoor play, which is essential for children's physical development.

According to research conducted outside Korea on outdoor play, children who grew up playing outdoors developed faster physically, were able to concentrate better, and were less frequently sick; also, their play was more diverse, imaginary and creative (Moore, 2000, cited in Lee Boo-mi, 2001: 86). In studies conducted in Korea, it was also revealed that children who engage in outdoor activities almost everyday were more sociable than children in childcare who did not have such programs (Woo Namhee & Koo Hyuna, 2000).

Outdoor activity is viewed as an integrated sphere in which all six areas of development listed in the standard childcare procedure can take place. As shown in Table 7.4 (below), many day care centres in Korea do not have an adequate number of teachers and assistants, often limiting the capacity for children to have outdoor activities. However, there are around 300 childcare facilities that are part of Children's Houses for Cooperative Childcare or the Eco-Infant Cooperative, both of which have major programs that include outdoor field trips, walks, and growing vegetables, in contrast to all other childcare facilities, where such outdoor activities do not take place.

Day care centres in private homes or shopping malls that are licensed have fewer than 20 children, but do not necessarily have a garden. In larger facilities, the situation is not much different because there is no law stipulating that there have to be outdoor play areas. Consequently a child may stay inside all day, and in some cases into the night too, giving rise to a serious policy issue about the quality of child care. The standard childcare procedures currently under development should clearly specify the percentage of outdoor activities that should be compulsory or should specifically nominate compulsory outdoor activities. If outdoor activities are included as a daily requirement, the teacher-child ratio must be reduced, which means the number of teachers in day care centres must be increased.

Table 7.4 (following) shows child-teacher ratios in the three types of cooperative day care centres where high quality education takes place. These centres are part of a work-based consortium with extensive support from companies and from existing day care centres.

Table 7.4. Child vs. Teacher ratio

Age (month)	Existing day care centre	Cooperative childcare	Consortium type day care centre at work	Paedology (age x 3)
1~12	1:3	1: 2~3	1:3	1: 2~3
12~24	1:5	1: 3	1:4	1: 3~6
24~36	1:7	1: 5~7	1:6	1: 6~9
36~48	1:15	1: 7~10	1:11	1: 9~12
48~60	1:20	1: 10~13	1:14	1: 12~15
After school hours	1:20	1: 13		

(Sources: Ministry of Gender Equality & Families (2004), Cooperative childcare and Communitarian Education (2000), Statistics about the consortium type at work are from telephone interviews.)

Low quality services in day care centres, as discussed above, encourage parents to turn to additional educational institutions. Stay-at-home mothers collect their children from day care centres at around

2 to 3 pm and send them to other educational institutions. Children of working mothers also leave day nurseries before closing hour and go to other institutions. For example, 46.5 per cent of children of working mothers and 30.1 per cent of children of non-working mothers attend more than two nursery/educational services (Seo Mun-hee et al, 2005: 101). Stay-at-home mothers certainly have more time to look after children's study by themselves than working mothers, which drives the latter to have their children engaged in more educational programs.

Considering that Korea is a highly educated society where almost half the high school graduates enter college (45.4 per cent in 2004), a key policy consideration should be to improve the educational skill of nursery teachers. Investment in retraining teachers and in increasing their numbers is required. This in turn requires an increase in the government's childcare support budget. As mentioned in the above Ministry of Gender Equality and Family research, childcare costs would need to increase by 2.5 to 3.5 times to improve the quality of childcare (Park Gi-baek et al, 2005).

Increased costs would place pressure on parents. In 2004, average monthly nursery and education expenses for preschool children were W235,000 (US$235), with the lowest being W3000 (US$3) and the highest W1,440,000 (US$1440). Average monthly nursery and education expenses for one child were W172,580 (US$173) (the expenses includes that for children who received a fee waiver or discount), and for two children, twice the amount, at W344,840 (US$345.) Average monthly nursery and education expenses for children in the care of in-law relatives was W445,200 (US$445), with a standard deviation of W250,500 (US$250) (Seo Mun-hee et al, 2005: 118, 121, 313). Among additional expenses for extra education programs, childcare subsidies (44.7 per cent) takes the highest priority, followed by diversity of available programs (18.2%), by those surveyed (Seo Mun-hee et al, 2005: 387).

As a percentage of GDP, child care/child education costs per child in 2001 in Korea were low at $US1913 compared to the OECD average of US$41871. The percentage of GDP for providing support to childcare/child education facilities for children over three years of age was 0.1 per cent in Korea compared to the OECD average of 0.4 per cent (OECD, 2004a, b). If the absence of family allowances in Korea is also taken into account, the gap becomes even bigger. In European countries that have successfully avoided low birth rates, the family allowance alone is 1.5 per cent (Grant J et al, 2004, cited by Lee Jae-gyeong, 2004). However, in Korea, despite the government's recognising the low birth rate as a national strategic crisis and despite its major policy initiative to combat this low reproductive rate, the total budget for the government's 'comprehensive measure to combat low birth rate' for 2005 and 2006 came to a mere 0.2 per cent of GDP (Table 7.6). This is only seven to 13 per cent of what European governments pay in family allowances alone. By 2009, Korean families will receive up to 130 per cent of the average urban working class income in childcare subsidies, and 80 per cent of all children in Korea will receive government subsidies for their care. However, the budget ratio in terms of GDP is unlikely to change. In comparison to 2006, the total budget will have only doubled to 4.662 trillion (Joint Response by related Ministries and Organisations, 2005). If, in the process, the childcare fee structure is deregulated in order to normalise the quality of childcare services, and if the parents' share of the costs increases, it may render government efforts to combat the low birth rate meaningless.

Table 7.5 National government budget for combating low birth rate in GDP percentage (unit : a hundred million won, %)

	Total budget for combating low birth rate (a)	Forecasted GDP (KDI)(b)	The GDP rate of total budget for combating low birth rate (a/b x 100)
2005	16,912	831,3788	0.20
2006	23,351	898,7205	0.26

(Source: Joint Response by related Ministries and Organisations (2005), KDI(2005), Hyundai Economic Research Institute (2005).

Family participation in child care

In a survey on low birthrate, conducted amongst 1054 married and unmarried young people (male 467, female 587), 3.2 out of every 10 adults aged between 20 and 40 said that women avoid childbirth because 'childbirth and child care all fall on women', and 2.7 said that 'no help is available for child care' (Reasons why we do not bear children, http://www.womennews.co.kr/news/view.asp?num=26288). Also, out of 9303 people who took parental leave in 2005, only 181 were male workers (Ministry of Labour, 2005). Furthermore, women in paid work continue to have similar responsibilities for housekeeping as non-working women: average housekeeping per day for women is three hours and 18 minutes, while for men it is 26 minutes (KNSO, 2004b). This demonstrates that female workers cannot expect much from their husbands when it comes to sharing the housework. Thus, for full-time female workers, the total daily work hours on average, including housework, is 12–13 hours. Women find it very hard to cope with such a heavy 'double' workload, as is clear from the following statements:

> "It was physically very challenging, which led to severe depression."
>
> "Having no personal life, it feels like three years had passed when it's only been three months."
>
> "With my first child, I had a difficult time with my mother (who was taking care of it) and the baby was ill all the time. I really wanted to quit my job, wondered what on earth I was doing..."
>
> "Being a reporter is practically impossible. To spend more time with kids, I'm thinking of moving to a job with regular working hours"
>
> (Kim Jeong-hee et al, 2004: 73–74)

Table 7.2 (above) showed that 44.5 per cent of working mothers received help from blood relatives and 4.7 per cent from non-related people. Women who received support from their own mothers or mothers-in-law expressed guilt about being a bad daughter by burdening their parents with the care of their own children (Kim Jeong-hee et al, 2004: 69-79). For the older generation of carers, the situation is also unsatisfactory. It seems to me that older people do not take comfort in taking care of their grandchildren. Given the conflicts that arise, child care by relatives is often not a desirable alternative.

In 2006, the Korea Youth Corps (KYC), whose members are workers, housewives and college students mainly in their 20s and 30s, held a press conference asking for the introduction of a 'Papa Quota', under which fathers would be automatically given a certain period of leave for child care, and declared they would wage a 'baby strike' until the end of the year (to reclaim fatherly lover, http://www.hani.co.kr/arti/society/labor/153919.html). The press conference is testimony to evolved, younger generations in Korea who are willing to share the responsibility of child-rearing. It is government policies that are lagging behind.

Programs such as 'Daddy Month' in Sweden and 'Papa Quota' in Norway pay fathers to take paternity leave. Those fathers who developed a primary bonding relationship with their child by helping their wives immediately after childbirth continued to participate voluntarily in child care activities (Kim, Mihwa, 1990). Feminist psychologists observe that parentally gender-segregated child care tends to regenerate gender stereotype: girls to have relation oriented ego and boys more individual and atoministic or chauvinistic ego, which reinforces patriarchy (Chodorow, 1978; Dinnerstein, 1989.) If it is urgent to combat the low birth rate in Korea, it is also necessary to introduce paternity leave options similar to those in Sweden and Norway as soon as possible. Compulsory paternity leave may have a revolutionary effect by transforming men who say that they agree with participating in child care in principle but who do not practise what they believe.

The need for 'night nursing' should be reviewed as a key cultural transformation. Night nursing is the extension of child care beyond normal office hours, for example between 7 and

10 pm, for parents who work late. Night nursing facilities in Korea have increased from 600 in 2004 to 2000 in 2005, and the government plans to continue to increase this number. However if the government continues to support funding night-time childcare without changing the long-working hour culture, no changes will occur in the labour system or in fathers' participation in child care. It is possible, even with current long working hours, to decrease the demand for night-time child care if couples cooperate with each other and take turns in working night hours, or if Korean society supports the development of such a culture.

The need for night nursing comes from the fact that mothers cannot expect fathers to take responsibility for feeding infants at night, and they also cannot expect any social support for such sentiments. The absence of campaigns to encourage fathers to leave work on time will further turn Korea into a work- and male-centred society, and women who are only now beginning to express their desires for social achievements, which had been denied to them before, will continue to avoid childbirth and child care.

Lastly, it may be worth reviewing the possibility of operating and co-locating childcare facilities with older people's day care centres (known as 'elderly pavilions'). However, at the individual household level, relying on older grandparents for child care, as discussed above, is not very promising as a sustainable child care plan.

Conclusion

Female workers with children are 'sandwiched' between their children's and their elderly parents' generations. Their effort to balance child care and education with their job is almost as if they are in a constant battle field. This chapter has attempted, through analysing a wide range of data, to demonstrate what the reality is for such women. We have argued that women's perception of child care as a burden, and education has led to unprecedented low birth rates in Korea. The government has only recently recognised that child care is a core national priority and that social reproduction requires economic investment. However, the child care and child education 'war' in

Korea cannot be solved by economic investment alone (particularly given that the size of such investment in Korea is far below that of European countries, which are also fighting to counter low birth rates). The importance of changing the patriarchal culture, which is integral to the phenomenon of low birth rates, has not been given due consideration in government policy. Fathers' parental leave and a system for fathers to leave work on time are two practices that must become mandatory up to a certain point if the government is genuinely seeking to promote a successful birth-friendly and family-friendly work culture. Otherwise, policies will remain ideological slogans rather than practical solutions.

The government must make efforts to introduce and stabilise a culture of gender-inclusive child care, where both mothers and fathers are actively involved, rather than allow the culture of gender-segregated child care to continue; otherwise the attitudes of young women workers, and men who agree with them, will not change. It is young Korean working women, who are fertile, who consider traditional family values to be anachronistic. Many such women have resolved that success or failure in life comes from their work outside the home. Government policy should make bi-parental child-rearing a basic practice. Equally important are single-parent households, remarriage households, and grandparent-grandchildren households. Government policies should consider these households as equally important when they develop any policy on child care. Government policies must also include programs for introducing gender-equal and multi-cultural child care. Also required are family allowances that could supplement the limitations of the current childbirth leave system, a realistic personnel replacement system, and the improvement of child care quality from an ecological perspective.

References

Ministry of Labour, 2005. A Survey on Basic Wage Structure. Seoul.

Chodorow N, 1978. The Reproduction of Mothering. Berkeley: University of California Press.

Collecting opinions on running a bank for replacement manpower, http://www.csc.go.kr/community/ForumView01.asp?siid=22&bbs_id=36&thisPage=/community/Com0501.asp&brd_id=22, access date: 15. March 2005.

Cooperative Childcare and Communitarian Education, 2000. Guideline for Communal Childcare. Seoul.

Dinnerstein D, 1989. Survival on Earth. In J. Plant,ed Healing the Wounds. Philadelphia: New Society Publishers.

Grant, Jonathan, et al, 2004. Low Fertility and Population Ageing, RAND EUROPE.

Hyundai Economic Research Institute, 2005. 2006 Economic Forecast, Seoul.

Hwang Soo-kyong, 2004. Part time work and Use of female labor power. Seoul: Korea Labour Institute.

I am scared that I would hear 'why don't you take the parental leave?, hani.co.kr 6 Oct 2002, access date: 8. Nov 2002.

Joint Response by related Ministries and Organisations, 2005. Joint Report by related ministries-Child birth with father and Childcare policy, Seoul.

KDI, 2005. KDI Economic Forecast 2005 ¾, Seoul.

Kim Jeong-hee, 1998. Bio-feminism: an ontological study on the basis of Buddhism and Taoism. PhD Ewha Womans University, Seoul.

Kim Jeong-hee, et al, 2004. Survey on the demand for extended care service and suggestions. Seoul: The Ministry of Gender Equality & Family.

Kim Jeong-hee, 2005a. The Present and Prospect of Bio-Feminism. Seoul: Prun Sasang.

Kim Jeong-hee, 2005b. Bio-Feminist Ethics in the Lives of Buddhist Women: A Little Emancipation at a Time. Asian Journal of Women's Studies, VOL 11. No. 3.

Kim Jeong-hee, 2005c. Bio-Feminism in the Korean Society in the Age of Globalization. Paper presented at 'Women's Worlds 2005: 9th International Interdisciplinary Congress on Women' in Seoul, Korea.

Kim Jeong-won and Kim Il-ok, 2005. The Realm of Standard Childcare Process. Material Collection for Public Hearing about Standard Childcare Process, The Ministry of Gender Equality and Family, Seoul.

Kim Mihwa, 1990. A Study on the Sexual Division of Labour in Working Class Family: The Case of Male Participation in Childcare, Master's Thesis, Ewha Womans University, Seoul.

KNSO – see Korea National Statistical Office

Korea National Statistical Office, 2003, Annual Report on Vital Statistics. Seoul.

Korea National Statistical Office, 2004a, Annual Report on Vital Statistics. Seoul.

Korea National Statistical Office, 2004b. A survey of everyday life. Seoul.

Korea National Statistical Office, 2004c. Guidebook of Survey of Economically Active Population. Seoul.

Korea National Statistical Office, 2005. Annual Report on the Economically Active Population Survey. Seoul.

Lee Boo-mi, 2001. Children's experience of nature in the picnic. Children and Nature(presented paper in The 20th anniversary conference on nursery education being hosted by Korean Association for the Fostering and Education of the New Generation).

Lee Jae-gyeong et al, 2005. Low Fertility: Gender Analysis and Policy Implications. Seoul: Presidential Commission on Ageing Society and Ministry of Health and Welfare.

Lee Mihwa et al, 2005. Status of Childcare Nationwide 2 : A Research on the Actual Conditions of Nursing Facilities. Seoul: The Ministry of Gender Equality & Family.

Ministry of Labour, 2004. Almanac on Employment Insurance Statistics, Seoul.

Ministry of Labour, 2005. White Book of Labour. Seoul.

Moore R C, 2000. Children Immersed in Nature. Paper presented at 8th International Academic Conference on Nursery Education: Children, Environments and Safety being hosted by Samsung Welfare Foundation.

OECD – see Organisation for Economic Co-operation and Development

Organisation for Economic Co-operation and Development, 2004a. Education at a glance.

Organisation for Economic Co-operation and Development, 2004b. Indicators.

Organisation for Economic Co-operation and Development, 2006. OECD Employment Outlook.

Park Gi-baek et al, 2005. A study on standard nursery expense and appropriate nursery expenses. Ministry of Gender Equality and Family, Seoul.

Park Hyon-sok, 2005. Family Policies of the overseas couTgwntries Finland – baside maternity leave, 158 days parents leave is available, http://moge.news.go.kr/warp/webapp/news/view?section_id=a7_sec_1&id=057828f46f1df381c20c4f86, access date: 11 April 2005.

"Reason why we do not bear children", http://www.womennews.co.kr/news/view.asp?num=26288' access date: 10 Oct 2005.

Seo Mun-hee et al, 2005. Status of Childcare Nationwide1 : A Study on the use and demand for childcare facilities 2004, Minister of Gender Equality & Family.

"To reclaim fatherly love", http://www.hani.co.kr/arti/society/labor/153919.html, access date: 10 Sep 2006.

Woo Namhee and Koo Hyuna, 2000. A study on the development of children's pro-social behaviour: children's helping and sharing behaviour. Study of Domestic Science Vol. 5. Seoul: Domestic Science Institute of Dongduk University.

8

Health, economic, and policy implications of an ageing Australia.

Hal Kendig and Ruth Phillips

Introduction

Lifespan, generational relationships, and the context of social change are key issues for policy on ageing in Australia. This chapter will examine how ageing has been addressed as a social policy issue in Australia as well as exploring, to some extent, how older people are constructed as a group for research and policy development in Australian society. First, the specific characteristics of the Australian context will be discussed. Second, key areas of ageing policy will be examined, including costs and economic futures, health and care futures. Third, some issues concerning attitudes towards ageing and ageing policy in Australia will be raised.

Australia in context

Australia is a comparatively stable society and population ageing has been relatively moderate, with the most notable change being the recent rapid increase in the number of people in Australia of 80 years of age and over (Kendig, 2000: 107–111). For example, the number of Australians over 85 years of age increased by 114 per cent over the past two decades, from under one per cent in 1984 to 1.5 per cent in 2004 (ABS, 2006d). As noted by McDonald in Chapter 2 in this book, the rate of population ageing in Australia will increase. This shift in Australia's demography has resulted in a growth in both social policy responses and services development. However, many of Australia's ageing policies are bound up in conflict and tensions between the national Commonwealth government and the various state governments over the implementation of policies. Negotiations between the Commonwealth and State governments are at the centre of many of Australia's ageing policy issues. As argued by Phillips in Chapter 1, a further and very important contextual point is that while many countries in Asia are building up their welfare states, arguably

Australia's welfare state is contracting under the current Howard government that has been in power for more than a decade.

At the societal level, Australian family values and family relationships are generally characterised by a strongly suburban culture. This is an important contrast to many Asian social contexts. Family relations in Australian society are also dominated by the idea of 'intimacy at a distance', in which generations within families live in separate households while maintaining strong emotional and social bonds. This is related to a culture of dispersed families spread across low-density urban areas and also to the material capacity of families to stay apart but keep in touch. As a basic standard of living, most Australians have access to sufficient financial resources, transport and telephone services necessary for this form of family relationship (Kendig, 2000:111). Despite this factor of distance, older Australians enjoy strong social networks and strong family bonds and draw heavily on (and contribute to) kinship-based intergenerational bonds; these relationships are often highly gendered with women more likely to hold together such links and relationships (Kendig, 2000: 112). This is strongly evident amongst divorced older men who tend break family ties and men who never marry who are likely to become socially isolated (Kendig, 2000:113).

Australia is a settler nation and continues to be a nation of immigrants, with one in every four Australians born overseas (ABS, 2006c), along with a small, socially disadvantaged and disproportionately young Indigenous population. This has led to complex cultural and language groupings, which means it is impossible to generalise the social experience of ageing across the entire Australian population.

The significance of Australia's ageing population

Ageing is becoming recognised as a social and economic issue of major national significance for Australia. This issue is linked to new expectations of longevity that have wide-ranging implications for social and economic policy in Australia (Borowski et al, 2007). The large baby boom cohort is entering later life at a time of a persistent low fertility rate as discussed by McDonald in Chapter 2. Based on

2006 statistics, people over the age of 65 comprised 13 per cent of the overall Australian population (ABS, 2006a) and current (2002–04) life expectancy for males, currently aged 50 years, is a further 31 years on average to age 81 years, which is an increase of 7.8 years since 1970–72 data was collected (ABS, 2006b). Female life expectancy at 50 years of age (2002-04) increased by 6.5 years over the same period and they can now expect to live an extra 35 years to almost 85 years of age (ABS, 2006b). These changes are largely attributable to a large decrease in mortality caused by cardiovascular disease as a result of lifestyle changes and improvements in medical care (AIHW, 2004: 357).

Indigenous Australians do not share in the increasing longevity and on the whole can expect to live 20 years less than their non-Indigenous counterparts due to the extremely high social, economic and health disadvantage they experience as a group in Australian society (Steering Committee for the Review of Government Service Provision, 2003).

The majority of older Australians report being in good to excellent health, as reflected in findings from the 2001 National Health Survey. Even in the 85 year and over group 72 per cent of males and 60 per cent of females believed they had good, very good or excellent health (AIHW, 2004: 359). This report goes hand in hand with the high number of older people living independently in their own homes and the large number of older Australians involved in volunteer work (AIHW, 2004: 361). However, due to increasing numbers of very old people, in 2002 Australia was home to around 162,000 people with dementia (0.8 per cent of the population) and these numbers will increase greatly to 2040 (Access Economics, 2003: 31).

The prospects for such long lives have wide-ranging implications because older age has become a major part of contemporary Australian healthy life. The OECD (2006) report *Live Longer, Work Longer* noted that from 1970 to 2004 the expected duration of retirement in Australia increased from 10.9 to 18.9 years for men, and from 12.4 to 21.2 years for women. As estimated by Khoo and McDonald (2003), people over the age of 65 are going to comprise a quarter of the Australian population by the middle of the century. The

Prime Minister's PMSEIC Committee (2003), on the basis of present scientific evidence, set a national goal to be achieved by mid-century for a further 10 years of healthy and productive life, not just another ten years of life per se.

Indeed, the World Health Organization (WHO) has recently published 'HALE at birth'[1] data at 60 years of age for all member states for 2002. Based on their findings, at 60 years of age, Australian males and females could expect an average additional 16.9 and 19.5 years of life, free of poor health respectively (ABS, 2006b). The Australian life expectancies are close to those countries ranked highest in the world for healthy ageing.

These healthy productive years over 60 are known as the 'third age' (Laslett, 1996: 4). The term 'third age' emerged in the 1970s after the emergence of the first 'university of the third age' was established in France and entered the broad English lexicon as an alternative way of describing active older people (Laslett, 1996: 3). The 'third age' is a way of making a distinction between active older age and the 'fourth age', a period of relative dependency now regarded as only a few years at the end of life or 'the age of decline' (Laslett, 1996: 5). This view of the ageing population is a departure from earlier theories and foci on a group of people who, rather than 'disengaging' or falling victim to a society that excludes them, 'finds itself in a position of greater potential agency' (Gilleard & Higgs, 2002: 370). Although the focus of Laslett's (1996) recognition of this group is based on a newly found freedom as pensioners (not working) and a level of moral individualism that has spawned a huge market for a specific cohort of active aged consumers, this is clearly not the case for everyone. A number of Australians are retiring to find themselves with insufficient incomes to live well. Indeed, a key pressure of an ageing population is the capacity of the diminishing younger population to sustain at least partial financial support for the majority of older people who have not accumulated sufficient superannuation or retirement savings to pay for their own support through old age (Kelly & Harding, 2006). It is

[1] "HALE" – Healthy Adjusted Life Expectancy

projected that the government funded Age Pension expenditure will reach 4.6 per cent of gross domestic product by 2050 (ABS, 2005b).

An important contributing factor to the 'cost of an ageing population' in Australia is that labour force participation of people in the third age currently is relatively low, with only around half of men and about a quarter of women between 60 and 64 years of age (ABS, 2004) working in paid employment. Of this group 21 per cent work part-time and 57 per cent of that group are women, reflecting the greater overall *part-time* participation rate of mature aged women in the workforce (ABS, 2004). Low workforce participation for third age Australians is a crucial factor in key social policy areas and governments are taking action to encourage longer labour force participation for mature age workers, as discussed further below.

Home ownership is the mainstay of personal autonomy and financial security for the vast majority of older Australians. Multi-generational households are relatively rare in Australia and, in many cases, involve the adult children coming home to their parents, rather than the parents moving in with their children for support. The latter arrangement is declining due to older people's preferences to live independently and their economic capacity to do so (Kendig, 2000: 110). The overwhelming preference amongst older Australians and their adult children is to live in their own homes. In Australia in 2002–03, 83 per cent of older people lived in their own home, and 13 per cent lived independently in rented accommodation (ABS, 2005a).

It is important to emphasise that ageing in Australia involves diverse individuals as well as populations. Older Australians, like many older people around the world, generally feel that they are the person they have always been, and part of the ageing process is the struggle or challenge to maintain identity in adapting to ageing changes, and to adapt to a changing world. Current ways of looking at ageing emphasise individual agency and rely on the understanding of the importance of each older person's life course. For example, a generalised construction of old age as dependency is countered by the fact that only a small percentage (7 per cent) of older Australians, often only in their fourth age, are in need of high-level care or supported care outside of their own dwelling (ABS, 2005a).

As older people live longer, they have more possibilities to become more different from each other or as Settersten points out:

> We now have more, and healthier, years to spend in various roles and activities. As a result roles and activities may become more varied and their structure may become more complex. The result may be a more flexible life course in which age is less important in determining social roles and life experiences (2002: 62).

Understanding cohort differences is critical to appreciating individual and population ageing particularly during periods of social change. Cohort experiences are shared by members of a society born around the same time and this approach allows for unique ways of understanding ageing as it draws on historical knowledge of the opportunities and expectations embedded in the history of differing periods of time (Settersten, 2002: 60–61). At present those in advanced old age in Australia are typified by the stoicism and austerity arising from experiencing their formative childhood years during the era from WWI to WWII including the Depression.

The very large 'baby boomers' cohort of Australians (the more than four million Australians who were born between 1946 and 1961) began to turn 60 years of age in 2005. Some notable points have been made about this cohort, as they appear to have higher expectations than other age groups; the boomers have always been at the centre of Australian society at each stage throughout their lives. Baby boomers generally are bringing good health to later life, although the prevalence of chronic disease in midlife now presents a worrisome outlook for the future. Relatively few are expected to attain the 70 per cent replacement income set as the goal for maintaining standards of living after retirement (Kelly & Harding, 2006).

How baby boomers can achieve a retirement income that meets their expectations is a key policy question in Australia. In part, this situation has created an imperative for baby boomers to work longer, postponing retirement. However, the potential to work longer will depend upon future economic conditions, changed social attitudes and questions about inter-generational equity. This is recognised by the

Australian Government and was well-articulated by the then Minister for Ageing in reference to the 'baby boomer' generation:

> We need to redefine 'retirement'. Our focus should not be on retirement age and when that begins, but on what can we do and what activities can be accommodated in our lives beyond traditional retirement age.
>
> The challenge for employers is to better tailor or customise the final years of working life, at whatever age that might be. Work and retirement should merge into a transition phase with flexible hours, different work patterns, different jobs or levels of responsibility.
>
> We need to put in place a more structured winding down phase, a gradual withdrawal. Work and retirement should be regarded as a continuum (Bishop, 2005).

The views expressed by the Minister are at odds, to some extent, with a view reflected in recent research. Qualitative research shows that baby boomers foresee no alternative but to adjust their lifestyles in future to fit incomes reduced to the low old age pension in retirement (Quine, et al, 2006: 148). They feel that the government expects baby boomers to provide more for their own old age while they are still working, but many resent the fact that they do not have enough time to save very much before retirement (Hamilton & Hamilton, 2006).

Importantly, Australia does not have a strong record for enabling older people to stay in the workforce. The OECD (2006) reports that the average effective age of retirement in Australia is 63 years for men and 61 years for women. While there is generally not a mandated retirement age, most people retire thus well before 65 years, which had become a socially expected workforce exit point. This is the age when men become eligible for the means-tested Age Pension (for women it is now 62 years). Employers' negative perceptions of older workers also add to the difficulties of remaining in the workforce (Encel, 1997: 140–142).

In a discussion about generational change, it is important to emphasise that the future is uncertain. Many things will happen that we do not know about yet. Projections discussed here are based on assumptions that may not eventuate. However, it is a fact that currently in Australia there are approximately 125,000 people who enter the working age group *each year*; in the 2020s it is expected that this will be the number of people entering working age *over the entire decade*. On the one hand that can be seen as a problem. Where is Australia going to find the workers to keep the economy going? On the other hand it is saying that attitudes to older workers and opportunities for enabling older people to stay at work beyond current 'retirement' age will have to change for economic reasons. There is already some evidence of this trend with 6.1 per cent of men and 7.4 per cent of women among Age Pensioners supplementing their income through paid work in 2004. This compares favourably with earlier figures from 2000 which were 5.1 per cent for men and 6.2 per cent for women (Lim-Applegate et al, 2005: 14). In the overall population the proportions of people over 65 years who were in the paid workforce increased from 12.8 per cent in 2000 to 16.2 per cent in 2004 (Lim-Applegate et al, 2005: 14). Clearly this trend could lead to a greater proportion of older Australians funding their own retirement and a smaller number reliant fully on the Age Pension.

The 'costs' of the ageing population in Australia

In Australia most social and economic policy debates about the ageing population are framed in terms of costs to government. The costs are substantial but they are often overblown in political rhetoric. Political responses to the ageing population can be shrouded in a panic about how the cost of older people's dependency cannot be afforded by a diminishing younger population. There can be the implicit blaming or scapegoating of older people themselves for the demographic changes that other countries in Europe are already managing quite well. While an ageing society demands close social and policy attention, the facts show generally Australian society is well placed to adjust, in relative terms, to managing the fiscal impact of an ageing population (Jackson & Howe, 2003: 19; Productivity Commission, 2005). It needs to be appreciated that real incomes are projected to increase substantially in the years ahead. There is a case for some of this additional income to be directed to the support of the older cohorts who have had less advantageous economic prospects over the course of their lives.

The three key areas of cost associated with the ageing population are post-retirement income support, the health and medical needs of older Australians and the cost of care for the frail aged. Addressing these key social policy demands will require economic strategies, social adjustments and changes in attitudes about work and work participation and flexibility and innovation in social policy.

The age pension and post-retirement income

A major cost of an ageing population is the Australian Government funding of the Age Pension. In the 2005–06 Budget the Australian Government spent more than $A21 billion on support for the aged and approximately $20.8 billion of that was spent on direct transfers in the means-tested Age Pensions (FaCSIA, 2005: 123). The number of people to be supported through the Age Pension is projected to reach 5.1 million by 2051.

At present approximately 70 per cent of Australians aged 65 years and older have at least a part pension and this proportion has declined slightly over recent decades (Kendig et al, 2004). The ageing population has caused government concern about the cost of this level of support into the future as it is funded through direct transfers of taxation revenue. Specifically, in 2004, 1.9 million older Australians (72 per cent) were in receipt of old age pensions (Daniels, 2004). The age requirement to receive the old age pension for men currently remains at 65 years, and for women is being progressively raised to 65 years by 2014 (ABS, 2005b). This suggests that by 2051 spending on the aged pension would be more than double its present level. However, to put this means-tested expenditure into perspective, taxation concessions on superannuation cost the government foregone revenue far greater than the outlays on the pension.

Currently an individual living on the means-tested Age Pension, is receiving, on average, $A280 per fortnight and a couple $A360 (FaCSIA, 2005: 141). The Age Pension is based on a maximum payment of 25 per cent of average male weekly earnings, reflecting the disadvantage of a person who depends entirely on this austere allowance, particularly if they do not have the low costs of outright home ownership. In recognition of the low-income status of those reliant entirely on the Age Pension the Australian and state governments also provide a number of concessions and allowances. These include travel concessions, health costs concessions, telephone allowances and a utilities allowance (FaCSIA, 2005: 143). The total expenditure on these concessions reached $A143.9 million in the 2005–2006 Federal Budget (FaCSIA, 2005:143).

The main alternative to a state pension funded retirement that has evolved slowly over the last eighty years or so in Australia, is self-funded retirement, through superannuation. This took a great leap forward in 1983: as part of a deal with unions to improve the social wage for Australian workers, the then new Labor government supported the introduction of the Superannuation Guarantee which ensured that workers covered by awards were provided with contributions to superannuation by employers as a 3 per cent wage equivalent (Borowski, 2005: 51). In 1992 the Superannuation Guarantee became a compulsory employer superannuation scheme in an attempt to force Australians to save for more of their own later life. The current requirement is that all employers make a nine per cent of wages/salary contribution to each employee's superannuation fund. Prior to this it was only government employees who benefited from a state mandated retirement savings scheme (Drew & Stanford, 2003: 2).

As of July 2007, the Australian Government had implemented radical changes in the taxation of superannuation in order to encourage further savings to retirement and longer workforce participation after 60 years of age. Key features of the new legislation are large income tax concessions for contributions to superannuation; provision for transition to retirement allowing income from both pensions and wages from age 55 years onwards, and tax free receipt of superannuation payments after age 60 years. The life-long benefits of these tax concessions for middle and high-income earners far exceeds the value of the means tested pension for those on lower incomes. The benefits are designed to encourage more mature workers to continue working to at least to age 60 years and preferably later.

In an international study of 12 OECD countries, Australia was ranked first in its capacity to meet the challenges of the costs of an ageing population (Jackson & Howe, 2003: 19). The authors found that Australia showed the least vulnerability to the cost of retirement income, for example, because it had a relatively low cost pension scheme and it was shifting its emphasis from public to private retirement income insurance. It is important to note, however, that these findings on Australia are based on two important assumptions. First, they assume a steady fertility rate of 1.8 babies per woman in Australia. Second, they assume a trend towards reducing the relative size of government, mainly by shifting the cost of the ageing population away from state responsibilities towards more private sector solutions (notably self-funded retirement) and by sharply limiting health expenditure. These assumptions, based on a conservative ideology, underpin Jackson and Howe's optimism about the Australian Government's capacities to manage the costs of an ageing population. Their predictions assume a strong economic rationalist approach to policy continuing far into the future – a scenario that may or may not be the case.

Health and care costs

Health and medical services, aged care, and pharmaceutical benefits are policy areas where costs are likely to rise with Australia's ageing population. As more Australians become older, they will place more pressure on government expenditure by increasing demands for residential and other supported care and medical services.

Care of older people

As reported by the Australian Institute of Health and Welfare (AIHW), the total Australian, state and territory recurrent government expenditure on aged care services increased from around $A5 billion in 2000–01 to around $7 billion in 2003–04 (2005: 185). Consistently the largest area of expenditure in aged care is at the high need end of care which is residential aged care, representing 73 per cent of expenditure in 2003–04 (AIHW, 2005: 185). The second largest area of expenditure on care for older people is in the Home and Community Care Program (HACC) which cost around $1.2 billion in 2003–04 for capital and services (AIHW, 2005: 185). In the HACC program approximately $A900 million was spent on delivering services to people aged 65 and over (13 per cent of recurrent aged care expenditure) (AIHW, 2005: 185). Community care places and packages are the third main area of aged care expenditure, and in 2003–04 they accounted for 4.4 per cent of government expenditure on aged care services (AIHW, 2005: 185). In addition $326.9 million was spent on the Carer Allowance, with 4.5 per cent of that amount provided to carers who themselves were aged 65 and over (AIHW, 2005: 185). The National Respite for Carers program accounted for $101.5 million, and Veterans' Home Care including in-home respite accounted for $91.1 million of community care expenditure (AIHW, 2005: 185).

As discussed by Brennan in Chapter 6, many older people manage on their own at home, or with help from relatives and friends, while others rely on a range of care services or a combination of services and informal help. Government funded community care is the mainstay of aged care in Australia and the vast majority of older people will never enter residential care. In 1998 nearly 347,000 people aged 65 and over were living at home using informal unpaid care only and 507,000 were living at home with the support of formal care services; 72 per cent of the latter group of service users also were assisted by unpaid carers (AIHW, 2003a: 294). Five years later in 2003 there was virtually no change in the number of older people at home with only unpaid care (345,500) but the number with formal care service users had increased by 20 per cent to 607,100 (AIHW, 2003a: 294). Overall, the figures suggest that the use of community services was increasing at least as fast as the numbers of older people having severe or profound limitations in their daily lives living in the community. The greater policy emphasis on 'ageing in place' resulted in relatively fewer people remaining at home with only unpaid care.

In 2004, the government released 'A New Strategy for Community Care – The Way Forward' (DoHA, 2004). This strategy arose from the Review of Community Care Programs and was intended to ensure more consistency and coordination of program operations. Further, in response to an area of growing concern in aged care, dementia, the 2005 Australian Government Budget announced the creation of 2000 new dementia-specific 'Extended Aged Care at Home' places over the next four years (DoHA, 2004). A further response was to declare dementia as a National Health Priority given its increasing prevalence as the population ages and the effects it has on care needs.

Health

Government provides 90 per cent of health funding in Australia, with the remaining 10 per cent provided through private health insurers (AIHW, 2004: 228). Health expenditure is principally the responsibility of state governments (primarily for hospitals) with a considerable proportion of the expenditure being derived from direct transfers from the Australian Government (AIHW, 2004: 228). Even though it provokes much public debate, medical services are quite a small part of the overall costs of the ageing population. Total national expenditure on health in Australia was equivalent to 9.3 per cent of the GDP in 2000–2001, amounting to around $A67 billion (AIHW, 2004: 228). Australia spent around $3397 per person in 2001 compared to other members of the OECD such as the USA at $6548 at the highest end and Japan with $2291 at the lowest end of expenditure (AIHW, 2004: 241).

The other large area of health expenditure in Australia is in pharmaceuticals. Australians spent more than $A10 billion on pharmaceuticals in 2000–01, a significant increase from 9.9 per cent of the overall health expenditure in 1991–92 to 14.1 per cent in 2000–01 (AIHW, 2004: 237).

Overall health costs of older Australians are higher than those for the general population. Older Australians see doctors more often and longer, have higher rates of symptoms, medical and chronic conditions and were prescribed more medications, particularly in the over-75 age group (AIHW, 2004: 373). Older Australians stay in hospitals at twice the rate of the average population and utilise more than twice as much financial subsidies under Medicare (Australian

Government health insurance) than the rest of the population (AIHW, 2004: 377). The average health expenditure per person in 2000–01 was $A5509 for 65–74 year olds and $15,690 for people aged over 85 compared to $1807 for persons aged under 65 years (AIHW, 2004: 377). While this kind of data raises concerns for the costs of an ageing population, Australia in relative terms still does not spend a particularly large percentage of its overall GDP on health care for the older population (Productivity Commission, 2005). Further, there are reasonable prospects for health promotion that can maintain good health well into advanced old age (PMSEIC, 2002).

People with dementia are high end users of health care services (Access Economics, 2003). They go to the doctor more frequently than other Australians, and more often than others their own age. On average people with dementia stay in hospital twice as long as the general population. They incur emergency department costs two and a half times more than the general population along with a 50 per cent greater overall cost for hospital, medical and pharmaceutical needs. The greatest cost for people with dementia is in residential care, comprising 88 per cent of the overall health costs of dementia in Australia -- more than $A4 billion in 2003. Access Economics (2003) projects that this cost will double by 2011, leading to a need for stronger support within community care.

Future costs

The cost of the ageing population has informed a significant policy statement by the current Australian Government on this issue. The Intergenerational Report (IGR), prepared by the Treasurer as part of the 2002–03 Budget papers, provided projections on the fiscal costs to government of demographic change to the year 2045. This analysis makes basic assumptions that underpin the neo-liberal governance of the Howard government. Its focus was on cost, revenue, economic growth and reduction in the growth in government spending. Underlying the report are contested strategies of low government debt, maintaining an efficient and effective medical health system, widespread participation in private health insurance, containing growth in the Pharmaceutical Benefits Scheme, affordable and effective residential aged care system, preserving a well-targeted social safety net that encourages working-age people to find jobs and remain employed, encouraging mature age participation in the labour force and maintaining a retirement incomes policy that encourages private saving for retirement, and reduces future demand for the Age Pension (Treasurer, 2002). The most recent Intergenerational Report from the Australian Treasurer (2007) suggests that the fiscal impact of population ageing will be significant but less than had been anticipated in 2002.

When the first Intergenerational Report was released it heightened public concern about the ageing population and did not take much account of the many alternatives ahead for more constructive responses to population ageing. In particular, the IGR failed to consider the productivity and potential improvements in productivity among older Australians. It also did not discuss fully its own expectations for substantial increases in real incomes for Australians over the decades ahead. In 2005, a less politically driven government research report conducted by the Productivity Commission, while coming from a similar economic point of view, observed that "while the potential fiscal and economic consequences are great, population ageing does not currently represent a crisis" (Productivity Commission, 2005). The Commission concluded that the greatest risks ahead are to individuals having few financial resources on retirement. They recognised that the impact of the change in demographics is indeed slow and that there is capacity for the Australia economy and society to adjust to an ageing population.

Future policy implications

In examining the social policy options for addressing an ageing Australia, key areas will continue to arise. Concerns about income support and retirement income dominate policy analysis of this issue. These will be addressed in a number of ways. The rapid rise of privately funded superannuation – paid for primarily by employers and employees with generous taxation concessions – will see more self provision for old age by the more advantaged groups among the baby boomer cohort. However, the current compulsory rate of 9 per cent under the Superannuation Guarantee would have to be raised to around 15 per cent and made over 30 or 40 years of participation in the workforce for it to become a comprehensive alternative for all workers. This means that reliance on the Age Pension as a main source of income is set to continue for a considerable time into the future and the government is clearly planning for that cost. It should be noted, however, that Australia has yet to become a fully demographically mature society and it contributes relatively little towards the overall cost of its older population. In 2000, Australian Government expenditure on benefits for older people was around nine per cent, a low figure compared to the United Kingdom at 12 per cent or France at nearly 19 per cent (Jackson & Howe, 2003: 7).

Another important policy emphasis is on enabling older people to work longer. There are a variety of policies that are emerging incrementally. For example, under new transition to retirement provisions, people who would have otherwise retired are now able to draw from their superannuation benefits and continue to do paid work at the same time without being penalised. This reflects a harmonisation of work with income support. As older people are increasingly able draw on their wealth in various ways, as they will in the future, there will be a number of consequences, particularly if their savings and investments are dwindled in early retirement and completely diminished by the time they have 'frail age' needs.

The future of addressing the ageing of Australia are likely to see a mix of more public expenditure, increased self-provision and increased user charges. Questions about inter-generational equity will, however, continue. On the one hand the baby boomers cohort has been tremendously advantaged with its full exposure to benefits from the post-war era and they will carry those benefits through into old age in ways their parents never had. On the other hand, economic projections and recent experience in Australia point towards continued increasing productivity and a continuing rise in standards of living. Based on this scenario there appears to be no reason to exclude an older age cohort from Australia's future economic benefits and increasingly, key social policy issues will relate to individual economic status and economic security rather than age. In terms of social equity, the main concern is to draw on taxes and provide public benefits on the basis of need irrespective of the age of individuals.

In regards to the health outlook, there are some contrary trends. On the one hand there are trends towards improvements in health, especially in old age. However on the other hand, the chronic disease burden is building up to almost epidemic proportions in the baby boomer cohort through obesity and diabetes. There are notable increases in mental health difficulties with the rising burden of depression at younger ages and dementia at older ages. This means that in the mid-term future there are going to be major challenges. Rising health care costs in Australia, have so far been attributable more to higher utilisation of services, more use of technology and the costs of pharmaceuticals than to population ageing, It is of course important to accept that there are major demands in the multiple complex health and care difficulties particularly in the last few years of life. At very advanced old age there is a strong argument for a more balanced approach to care with a strong focus on quality of life and high quality palliative care as well as treatment and cure.

There is evidence of strong individual and public responses to these health challenges, along with increasing recognition of the value and great potential for healthy and active living. This includes the reduction in the number of older people smoking in Australia, due to a high quitting rate at younger ages and because many smokers die before they reach old age. Pharmaceutical expenditure has been a major area of cost increases over recent years, including considerable supply-driven demand, making it a major challenge to reduce expenditure on medication. In regard to rising health care costs it is important to ensure high-level access by older people to health care. Even though older people are major users of health care services, the major problem is the appropriateness of care and whether there is equity in access to care. A further, critical issue for Australia is the imperative to drastically address premature disease and death for Indigenous people. The health profile of Indigenous people in Australia is broadly similar to that in the most underdeveloped countries in the world.

Care in later life is expected to continue to focus on issues such as 'ageing in place', supporting older people in their own home with services that come to them rather than people going into residential care. The provision of residential care has been restrained over the past two of decades while community care has increased significantly. This system relies heavily on informal carers and their willingness and capacity to care, as most care of frail older people is provided through self-care and by spouses, daughters and other family members. There is also a rise in consciousness of the issue of consumer rights for the older population, with an increasing assertiveness, particularly in response to strong moves by government to user pays services. The increasing wealth of advantaged groups of older people will require new policy responses. However, as some recent research has shown most currently retiring Australians are not planning for the costs and needs of their frail age despite the promise of living longer; they still hold the view that the government should support their old age health and income needs (Quine, et al, 2006: 149). If this attitude drives political and government responses, the state will be required to commit more funds to pay for future frail age care needs.

Attitudes and directions

In conclusion, it is important to consider some of the bigger societal issues around an ageing population for Australia and for most other countries. It is very important to have a constructive approach to an ageing Australia and to critically analyse the 'ageing problem'. A great deal of research in this field is affected by attitudes and this is often reflected in the outcomes of that research. For example, ageism is particularly destructive to the potential of older people, and to the potential of an ageing society. Although a comparatively under-researched area compared to racism or sexism (Nelson, 2005: 208), there has been important international research that shows a very high level of ageism amongst younger people, reflecting global values of the valorisation of youth over age. Research also shows that the elderly stereotype is pervasive, crossing national and cultural boundaries (Cuddy et al, 2005) and as such is costly, constraining appropriate and effective policy responses in most countries. In Australia, qualitative research has shown that older people can be deeply affected by ageist attitudes, particularly among health professionals, that make them 'feel old' rather than normal ageing (Minichiello et al, 2000).

Research has shown that across cultures the mainstream society stereotype of older people is that they are warm but also incompetent – this is a mixed stereotype – both positive and negative. Research has also found that elderly people are viewed as possessing far fewer competence traits than warmth traits. Compared to younger people, elderly people have been rated as warmer and friendlier, but also as less ambitious, less responsible and less intellectually competent. In some recent USA research, regardless of gender, older people were rated as more feminine and less masculine than younger people and that young people are more likely to feel pity toward older people than admiration (Cuddy et al, 2005: 270). This has serious implications for maintaining older people's participation in the workforce and tapping into the rich resources of experience and knowledge that older people hold.

Ageism has been found to be all-pervasive across Eastern as well as Western cultures, including Confucian-based Asian cultures where respect for elders and filial piety are social norms (Cuddy et al, 2005: 273). As part of a large-scale international study, university students in Belgium, Costa Rica, Hong Kong, Japan, Israel (one Jewish sample and one Arabic sample), and South Korea rated elderly people and other groups on items measuring warmth and competence, status and competition. In all samples, participants viewed elderly people as significantly more warm than competent. Most interestingly, in the three most collectivist Asian samples – Hong Kong, Japan, and South Korea – this pattern held up (Cuddy et al, 2005: 273). In all samples, elderly warmth scores were significantly higher than views of people in the wider population and significantly lower than the overall view of competence in the wider population (Cuddy et al, 2005: 273). Researchers were surprised to find that East Asian participants reported broadly negative evaluations of elderly people (Cuddy et al, 2005: 274). In other cross-cultural investigations, participants in China, Japan, Taiwan and Thailand reported even more negative attitudes toward older people than their American counterparts. Widespread or global ageism is seen as a shift attributable to modernisation and the essential nature of capitalism that operates on individualist social views rather than traditional collectivist social views where older people have had equal or superior status in all types of groups or communities (Cuddy et al, 2005: 274). It is a core challenge to future policy makers to see older people as "individuals having their own preferences and their particular circumstances including their cultural and linguistic diversity" (Kendig et al, 2004: 19). Australian social policy will have to resist the globalised ageist trend and work toward improving regard for older people if it is to respect and utilise older people's capacities more effectively in the future.

The area of adequate income and work opportunities has little intrinsically to do with age but more with how age is interpreted in social policy and in labour markets. This should be where the policy is focussed. To address other key issues of ageing Australia will have to focus on improving general health over the entire life span, supporting independence in older age, and ensuring high quality care. This is an important, proactive approach for Australia, where ideas such as independence in old age and self-care continue to present challenges at personal and policy levels.

To seriously address the challenges of a change to a fully mature population – with many more older than younger people – it is important to enable social participation, and value all contributions in an aged friendly society. This means we should continually aim for 'a society for all ages' as emphasised by the United Nations in the International Year of Older Persons, 1999, where the key principles are that 'all age groups are equally worthy' and 'no age group should be discriminated against or especially favoured by society' (UN, 2000). The young of today are the old of tomorrow – those who are old now have a great generational stake in the future of the younger members of their families and communities. This provides an imperative to be inclusive in the way that we look at issues for ageing individuals and to ensure more appropriate social policy.

References

ABC (Australian Broadcasting Commission), 2006. Global Prevalence of Dementia. The Health Report [online]. Radio National,

Sydney: ABC. Available from: http://www.abc.net.au/rn/healthreport/stories/2006/1569392. htm# [accessed 24 April 2006].

Access Economics, 2003. The Dementia Epidemic: Economic Impact and Positive Solutions for Australia. Prepared for Alzheimer's Australia. Canberra: Access Economics. Available from: www.alzheimers.org.au/upload/EpidemicFullReport March2003.pdf

ABS – *see* Australian Bureau of Statistics

Australian Bureau of Statistics, 2005a. *Australian Social Trends 2005* [online], 4102.0. Canberra: ABS. Available from: http://www.abs.gov.au/ausstats/abs@.nsf/7d12b0f6763c78caca25706 1001cc588/4fe57db85b46d6cfca25703b0080cccc!OpenDocument [accessed 16 October 2006].

Australian Bureau of Statistics, 2005b. *Year Book Australia, 2005*, cat. no. 1301.0, Canberra: ABS.

Australian Bureau of Statistics, 2006a. *Australian Historical Population Statistics, 2006* [online], (3105.0.65.001). Australian Bureau of Statistics Web Site, Canberra: Commonwealth of Australia. Available from: http://www.abs.gov.au/AUSSTATS /abs@.nsf/DetailsPage/3105.0.65.0012006?OpenDocument [accessed October 2006].

Australian Bureau of Statistics, 2006b. Mortality and Morbidity, 4102.0 – *Australian Social Trends, 2006* [online]. Australian Bureau of Statistics Website, Canberra: Commonwealth of Australia. Available from: http://www.abs.gov.au/AUSSTATS/ abs@.nsf/Latestproducts/F7A76DCE3F8DC0A3CA2571B00013D99 C?opendocument [accessed October 2006].

Australian Bureau of Statistics, 2006c. One in every four Australians born overseas. *Media release* [online], 3412.0 – Migration, Australia, 2004-05 (last updated 29/03/2006). Available from: http://www.abs.gov.au/AUSSTATS/abs@.nsf/ mediareleasesbyReleaseDate/D90053C595C2C82ECA25713F007FF 258?OpenDocument [accessed October 2006].

Australian Bureau of Statistics, 2006d. Ageing Australians. *Year Book Australia, 2006* [online], cat. no1301.0. Canberra: ABS. Available from: http://www.abs.gov.au/ausstats/abs@.nsf/ Latestproducts/1301.0Feature%20Article62006?opendocument&tabname=Summary&prodno=1301.0&issue=2006&num=&view= [accessed October 2006].

Australian Bureau of Statistics, 2004. Paid Work: Mature Age Workers. 4102.0 – *Australian Social Trends, 2004* [online]. Australian Bureau of Statistics Website, Canberra: Commonwealth of Australia. Available from: http://www.abs.gov.au/Ausstats/abs@.nsf/46d1bc47ac9d0c7bca256c470025ff87/3c1b29bbc2c1d573ca256e9e00288ddf!OpenDocument [accessed April 2005].

AIHW – *see* Australian Institute of Health and Welfare

Australian Institute of Health and Welfare, 2005. *Australia's Welfare 2005* [online], Number 7. Canberra: Australian Government. Available from: http://www.aihw.gov.au/ publications/index.cfm/title/10186 [accessed April 2005].

Australian Institute of Health and Welfare, 2004. Australia's Health 2004. *The Ninth Biennial Report on the Australian Institute of Health and Welfare* [online]. Canberra: Australian Government. Available from: http://www.aihw.gov.au/ publications/index.cfm/title/10014 [accessed April 2005].

Australian Government, 2005. 'Shaping a Sustainable Future' Budget, 2005–2006 [online]. Canberra: Australian Government. Available from: http://www.budget.gov.au/2005-06/overview/html/overview_02.htm [accessed April 2005].

Bishop J, 2005. Opening Address to the 2nd International Conference On Healthy Ageing and Longevity. Speech by The Minister for Ageing, The Hon Julie Bishop MP [online], 2nd International Conference On Healthy Ageing and Longevity at the Brisbane Convention Centre, Brisbane, 18 March 2005. Available from: http://www.health.gov.au/internet/ministers/ publishing.nsf/Content/health-mediarel-yr2005-jb bissp180305.htm?OpenDocument&yr=2005&mth=3 [accessed May 2005].

Borowski A, Encel S and Ozanne E, 2007. *Longevity and Social Change in Australia*. Sydney: University of New South Wales Press.

Costello P, 2007. *Treasurer's Intergenerational Report 2007*. IGR2. Canberra: Commonwealth Government of Australia.

Cuddy A, Norton M and Fiske S, 2005. This Old Stereotype: The Pervasiveness and Persistence of the Elderly Stereotype. *Journal of Social Issues*, 61 (2), pp 267–285.

Daniels D, 2004. Social Security Payments for the Aged, People with Disabilities and Carers, 1909 to 1998. *Research Paper 11* [online], 1998–99. Available from: http://www.aph.gov.au/library/pubs/online/Aged.htm. [accessed 11 October 2006].

Department of Health and Ageing, 2004. *A New Strategy for Community Care: The Way Forward.* Canberra: The Department.

Encel S, 1997. Work in Later Life. In Borowski A, Encel S and Ozanne E, eds *Ageing and Social Policy in Australia*. Melbourne: Cambridge University Press, 1997.

FaCSIA (Department of Families, Community Services and Indigenous Affairs), 2005. Outcome 3 Seniors, People with Disabilities, Carers, Youth and Women are Supported, Recognised and Encouraged to Participate in the Community. *Portfolio Budget Statements 2005–06*, pp 119–160. Available from: http://www.facsia.gov.au/internet/facsinternet.nsf/aboutfacs/budget/budget2005-pbs.htm#budget [accessed October 2005].

Gilleard C and Higgs P, 2002. The Third Age: Class Cohort or Forum? *Ageing and Society*, 22, pp 369–382.

Hamilton M and Hamilton C, 2006. *Baby boomers and retirement: Dreams, fears and anxieties*. Discussion Paper Number 89. September 2006. Sydney: The Australia Institute. Available from: www.tai.org.au/index.php?option=com_remository&Itemid=36&func=select&id=2 – 31k

Kelly S, 2006. Mapping Behavioural Trends of the Baby Boomers. Demographic Destiny Report. Canberra: National Centre for Social and Economic Modelling University of Canberra.

Kelly S and Harding A, 2006. 'Retirement Incomes and Australia's Ageing Population', in Grewel B and Kummick M (eds.), *Engaging the New World: Responses to the Knowledge Economy*, Chapter 15, Melbourne University Publishing, Victoria, pp 357–73.

Kendig H, Gibson D, Harding et al, The Ageing of Australian Society: Economic, Fiscal and Societal Implications, Task Force report In Future Summit from the First summit, 6–8 May 2004, Melbourne: Australian Davos Foundation. Available from: www.pc.gov.au/study/ageing/subs/sub009.rtf

Kendig H, 2000. Family Change and Family Bonding in Australia. In Liu W and Kendig H, eds *Who Should Care for the Elderly?* Singapore: Singapore University Press, pp 107–123.

Jackson R and Howe N, 2003. *The 2003 Aging Vulnerability Index - An Assessment of the Capacity of Twelve Developed Countries to Meet the Aging Challenge* [online]. Washington DC: The Centre for Strategic and International Studies. Available from: http://www.csis.org/index.php?option= com_csis_pubs&task=view&id=888 [accessed April 2005].

Laslett P, 1996. *A Fresh Map of Life*. 2nd ed. Basingstoke, England: Macmillan.

Nelson T, 2005. Ageism: Prejudice Against Our Feared Future Self. *Journal of Social Issues*, 61 (2), pp 207–221.

Lim-Applegate H, McLean P, Lindenmayer P and Wallace B, 2005. New Age Pensioners – Trends in Wealth. *Conference Paper*, Australian Social Policy Conference, 20–22 July, Sydney, 2005, Seniors and Means Test Branch Department of Family and Community Services. Canberra: Australian Government. Available from: www.facsia.gov.au/research/austsocpolicy_ 2006/article1.htm

Minichiello V, Browne J and Kendig H, 2000. Perceptions and consequences of ageism: Views from older persons. *Ageing and Society* 2000, 20, pp 253–278.

OECD, 2006. *Live Longer, Work Longer: A synthesis report of the 'Ageing and Employment Policies' Project*. Paris.

Prime Minister's Science, Engineering and Innovation Council, 2003. Promoting Healthy Ageing in Australia. *PMSEIC Report*. Canberra: Commonwealth Government of Australia. Available from: www.dest.gov.au/.../publications_resources/profiles/ promoting_healthy_ageing_in_australia.htm.

Productivity Commission, 2005. Economic Implications of an Ageing Australia. *Research Report* [online]. Canberra: Australian Government. Available from: http://www.pc.gov.au/ study/ageing/finalreport/index.html [accessed May 2006].

Quine S, Bernard D and Kendig H, 2006. Understanding baby boomer's expectations and plans for their retirement: findings from a qualitative study. *Australasian Journal on Ageing*, 25 (3), pp 145–150.

Settersten R A, 2002. Social Sources of Meaning in Later Life. In R.Weiss and A. Scott, eds *Challenges of the Third Age, Meaning and Purpose in Later Life*. Oxford: Oxford University Press, 2002, pp 41–79.

Steering Committee for the Review of Government Service Provision, 2003. *Overcoming Indigenous Disadvantage: Key Indicators 2003 Report*, November 2003, Steering Committee for the Review of Government Service Provision. Canberra: Productivity Commission, Commonwealth of Australia.
Available from : www.pc.gov.au/gsp/reports/indigenous/ keyindicators2003/

Treasurer, 2003. Intergenerational Report. *Budget Paper Number 5, 2002–03* [online]. Available from: http://www.dfat.gov.au/budget/2002-03/bp5/html/03_BP5Part1.html#TopOfPage [accessed April 2005].

Treasury, 2005. *Fiscal sustainability and pre-funding strategies in OECD countries* [online]. Available from: http://www.treasury.gov.au/documents/1009/HTML/docshell.asp?URL=02_Fiscal_Sustainabiltiy_and_prefunding.htm [accessed April 2005].

UN (United Nations), 2000. Steps toward a Society for all ages. *International Year of Older Persons 1999* [online]. United Nations Website (last updated 31 May 2000). Available from: http://www.un.org/esa/socdev/iyop/iyoppre3.htm [accessed March 2005].

9

The health, economic, and policy implications of the ageing Korean society

Eun-jeong Kang

Introduction

The Korean population is changing rapidly in two respects. First, as the 'baby boomers' grow older, Korean society is ageing faster than any other country. Korea is expected to turn into an 'aged society' only 18 years after it became an 'ageing society'. In addition, rapid ageing in Korea is coupled with an unprecedented low fertility rate. Until two decades ago, Korea had propagated policies for lowering the fertility rate however now increasing the fertility rate is on top of the national policy agenda.

From a health perspective, rapid ageing means that the population's health is likely to get worse than in the past, as older people tend to spend a greater proportion on health care than other sectors of the population, and will continue to be high spending for their health care needs This implies that the Korean health care system needs to be reformed to provide sufficient care for the elderly.

In this chapter the dynamic changes in Korea's population as well as some of the efforts the government is making to deal with these changes will be addressed. It is hoped that this chapter will lead to active open discussions between Australia and Korea on the shared challenge of an ageing population.

Socio-economic characteristics of the Korean elderly

The proportion of elderly people in Korea in 2000 was 7.2 per cent, which is lower than in many developed countries.[1] However, the speed of ageing in Korea is striking. Table 9.1 shows that Korea will go from an 'ageing society' to an 'aged society' in only 18 years, and from an 'aged society' to a 'super-aged society' in only eight years. Coupled with the low fertility rate since the early 1990s, the old-age dependency ratio is expected to increase sharply.

Table 9.1. The age distributions and ageing indices of Korea

	1980	1995	2000	2005	2010	2018	2026
%	100.0	100.0	100.0	100.0	100.0	100.0	100.0
0~14	34.0	23.4	21.1	19.1	16.3	13.0	11.6
15~64	62.2	70.7	71.7	71.8	72.8	72.6	67.5
65 +	3.8	5.9	7.2	9.1	10.9	14.3	20.8
Old-age dependency ratio[2]	6.1	8.3	10.1	12.6	14.9	19.7	30.8
Ageing index[3]	11.2	25.2	34.3	47.4	66.8	110.3	178.7

Source: KNSO, 1996

Labour force participation of the elderly is high in Korea compared to many developed countries. In 2004, 29.8 per cent of persons aged 65 and over were engaged in economic activities (Korea National Statistical Office, 2004). In comparison, in 2001 the labour force participation rate of persons aged 65 and over in developed countries such as the US, UK, Canada and Australia was less than 10 per cent

[1] According to World Population Ageing 1950–2050 (UN, 2001), the percentage of people 65 and over in 2000 was 15.8 in UK, 12.3 in US, 11.7 in New Zealand, 17.2 in Japan, 16.4 in Germany, 12.6 in Canada, and 12.3 in Australia.

[2] Pop. 65 years old & over / 100 persons aged 15 to 64.

[3] Pop. 60 years old & over/100 persons under age 15.

(UN, 2001). The high participation rate of Korea's elderly reflects the weakness of the old-age income support system (including pensions and retirement programs).

The illiteracy rate of Korea's elderly was estimated to be 7.8 per cent among 65–69 year-olds and 12.5 per cent among 70 year-olds and over (UN, 2001). These estimates fare better than similar statistics in China or Singapore. The education level of the Korean elderly continues to improve.

Health status of the elderly in Korea

The average life expectancy increased from 70.8 in 1989 to 77.5 in 2003. As Table 9.2 illustrates, life expectancies at ages 65 and 80 are comparable to those of several OECD countries.

Table 9.2. Life expectancies at age 65 and 80

	Life expectancy at age 65		Life expectancy at age 80	
	Male	Female	Male	Female
Australia	17.6	21.0	7.9	9.7
Canada	17.2	20.6	7.9	9.8
Japan	18.0	23.0	8.3	11.0
Korea	14.9	18.7	6.6	8.1
United States	16.6	19.5	7.8	9.4

Source: OECD Health Data 2005

Even though general health continues to improve, improvements in the *quality* of health of older people is dubious. According to the National Health and Nutrition Survey (Figure 9.1 below), the subjective health status of adults overall has become better, but the subjective health status among the elderly has become worse. This is evident when the decline in the health status of the elderly is compared with the health status of young and middle-aged adults, which has improved substantially. Figure 9.1 (below) supports this analysis – it tells us that the subjective health status of the elderly needs more attention from policy makers and researchers.

Figure 9.1. Changes of subjective health status among the elderly

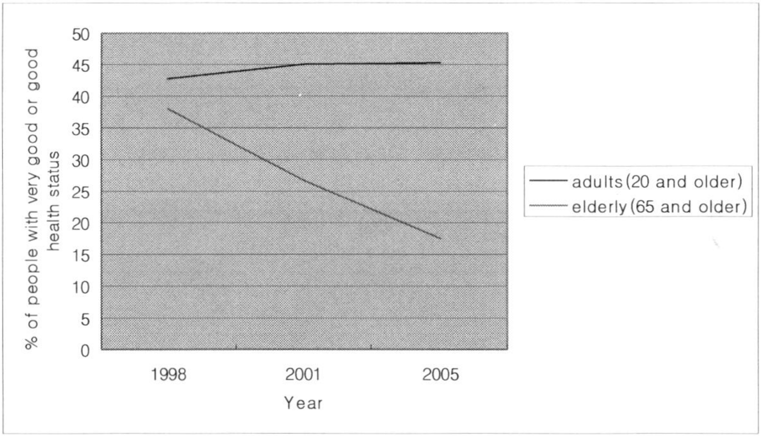

Data source: 1998, 2001, 2005 National Health and Nutrition Survey, Ministry of Health and Welfare

In many developed countries, including Australia, where the government has long intervened on behalf of the elderly, the health status of the elderly is now improving. In these countries, ageing does not necessarily mean higher medical expenditure or costs. However, if the Korean Government does not start to develop appropriate ways to improve the health condition of the elderly, ageing will place heavy economic burdens on current and future generations.

Given the lack of attention to the quality of health for older people as a core social policy issue in Korea, it is not surprising that Korea's elderly have many chronic diseases, because chronic diseases are related to a lower subjective health status (Leinonen et al, 1998). Some of the most prevalent chronic diseases are arthritis, hypertension, osteoporosis, and diabetes (Figure 9.2 below). The pain suffered from arthritis negatively affects the overall quality of life and health care costs for hypertension and diabetes were ranked the first and the third highest among various diseases in Korea in 1999. Both the visible and invisible costs of such chronic diseases are largely borne by elderly themselves whereas society should also bear the cost. (Kim et al, 2003). In order to enhance elderly people's quality of life and reduce the economic burden of managing disease, early interventions for preventing chronic diseases are required.

Figure 9.2. Prevalent chronic diseases among the elderly

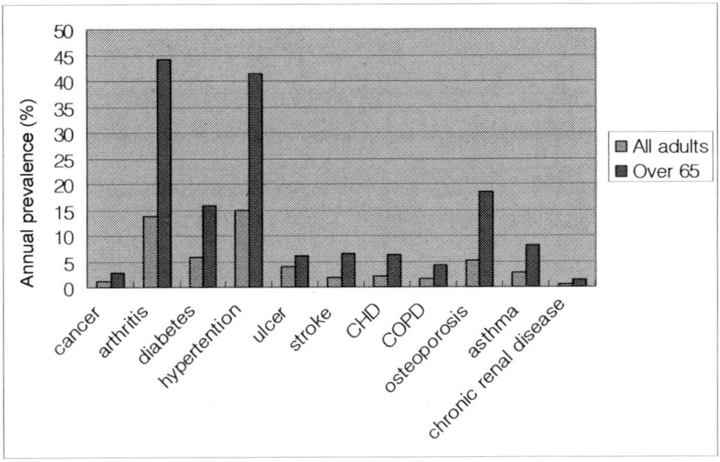

Data source: 2005 Health and Nutrition Survey, Ministry of Health and Welfare

Economic burdens from the health care services for the Korean elderly

Health care expenditure as a percentage of GDP in Korea is about six per cent, which is relatively small compared to that of other OECD countries. One of the mechanisms by which Korea has been able to control health care expenditure is via its national health insurance system whereby physician fee schedules and hospital reimbursement rates have been determined by the government.[4] However, for older people macro-efficiency through government regulation is difficult to endure given the rapidly rising medical costs. One of the reasons for rapidly rising medical costs is the increase in the elderly population, which has greater medical needs than other age groups.

In 2002, although the proportion of the elderly was only about seven per cent, the proportion of health care expenditure on the elderly ranged from 15 to 26 per cent. In particular, expenditure on inpatient care for the elderly is increasing faster than the proportion of the older population. Rising inpatient costs may be due to both the provider's practice fees and the higher demand for services brought on by the deteriorating health status of the elderly. Since about 80 per cent of health care providers are from the private sector, and physician fees are based on a fee-for-service principle, they are likely to provide unnecessary and/or expensive services. Assuming that the health care needs of the elderly will not decrease in the near future, strong governmental intervention is necessary if this trend in health care expenditure is to be reversed.

Figure 9.3. Total, inpatient, and outpatient health care expenditures of the elderly

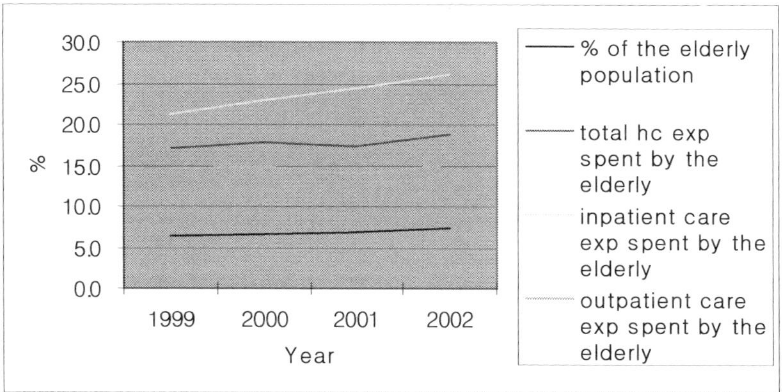

However, fee schedules are decided from 2001 by the negotiation between the government (National Health Insurance Corporation) and a group of medical and pharmaceutical representatives.

Data source: Statistics of National Health Insurance, National Health Insurance Corporation, 2003.

The rapidly rising inpatient costs for the elderly are also related to a lack of long-term care facilities. Many chronically ill elderly patients, who otherwise would have been admitted to a less costly long-term care facility, are admitted to acute care hospitals. Existing long-term care facilities are mainly for the indigent. Only 0.2 per cent of the elderly in Korea received institutional services in 2000 (OECD, 2005). Although there is poor data on the amount of long-term care expenditure in Korea, the OECD has estimated that about 0.3 per cent of GDP goes to long-term care (OECD, 2005). Among OECD countries, long-term care expenditure on average is 1.25 per cent of GDP.

The lack of long-term care facilities means that long-term care is usually provided informally at home. Even though its true that many older people in Korea would prefer to stay at home rather than be admitted to a residential facility, they often do not have the *choice* to do anything but stay at home. Furthermore, relying on informal care can be problematic, especially for those who need help but live alone (Jeong et al, 2001). The number of elderly people living in a one-person household increased from 8.9 per cent in 1990 to 16.2 per cent in 2000 (Korea National Statistical Office, 2004). Over the same period, the number of elderly living in a three-generation household decreased from 49.6 per cent to 30.8 per cent, reflecting a widespread shift away from extended family living.

Women have greater responsibilities than men when it comes to providing informal care for the elderly. A national survey showed that 74.3 per cent of caregivers were females in Korea (Jeong et al, 2001) and they too have health and welfare needs Almost 60 per cent of caregivers reported that their health was not good, and 10 per cent even had health conditions that limited their care activities. Generally caregivers had received no help for their own health problems (31.4 per cent) nor for errands or shopping (41.3 per cent). Therefore, in addition to the need for more long-term care facilities, there is a great need for housekeeping services, day care, respite care, and bathing services for family caregivers as well as the elderly.

Korea's strong family values play an important role in family care giving. Ninety-two percent of caregivers regarded caring for an older family member as their children's responsibility, and 80 per cent of them thought that such a sacrifice contributed to the harmony of their family. However, as nuclear families and women's economic participation increase, these strong family-oriented values are likely to be undermined (Jeong et al, 2001).[5]

Recent long-term care policies in Korea

The government has been making efforts to adapt to the rapidly ageing population, even though Korea is not an aged society yet. As mentioned above, the Korean Government recognises that we cannot rely on family caregivers any more, because of the increase in nuclear families and women's economic activities. In response, the current administration is taking two major steps to develop a better long-term care policy.

The so-called 'Elderly Care Act' was proposed in 2006 and was subject to a period of public scrutiny. This law is expected to be enacted in 2007 and to be effective from 2008. The purpose of the 'Elderly Care Act' is to improve the quality of life of the elderly and to reduce the burden on families. The target group includes the elderly as well as those who are younger than 65 but have 'geriatric diseases' such as dementia and stroke.

To finance additional care services for the elderly, a separate health insurance premium will be levied from people who participate in the national health insurance scheme. Fifty per cent of the budget for elderly care will come from this premium, 30 per cent from general tax revenue, and 20 per cent from individuals' out-of-pocket payments. Low-income families will be able to use elderly care services at a reduced out-of-pocket rate.

---

[5] The current issue of the low fertility rate is evidence of this change in values.

The National Health Insurance Corporation will be responsible for the management and operation of these elderly care services. Its responsibilities will include screening people who enrol in the scheme, collecting premiums, reviewing and subsidising fees, approving care facilities and disseminating information about them. The 'Elderly Care Act' supports the principle of 'consumer choice' in the selection of benefits and provides for as many kinds of benefits as possible. The services it covers include home care, institutional care, and care allowance.

A further issue is the need to maintain the quality of elderly care services. A national study is currently underway by the Korea Institute for Health and Social Affairs that aims to develop appropriate tools for evaluating the quality of health of users of elderly care services. Another study is being planned to test the feasibility and acceptability of the tools in practice. However, it is not clear at this stage how to carry out monitoring the quality of care and to reflect the quality indicators to the reimbursement for providing services.

A second major step for improving long-term care for the elderly is an effort by the National Health Insurance Corporation to increase the number of long-term care facilities, which will be in great demand when the 'Elderly Care Act' becomes effective. Starting in 2005, the National Health Insurance Corporation has been increasing the number of long-term care facilities by 100 per year. In addition, homes support services such as home-visit caregivers, caregiver vouchers and monetary assistance for low-income long-term care users will be also provided. However, it has not been decided which professionals will provide which long-term care services; therefore it is not easy to predict what the demand for certain professionals will be.

Even though the government's initiatives to improve long-term care for the elderly are promising, there remain many unresolved challenges that Korea will have to deal with in the near future. These challenges can be summarised as: continuity of care, quality control, and financial security.

The current Act fails to specify how medical care services and long-term care services will be seamlessly provided. Since long-term care insurance is separate from the health insurance, it is debatable which insurance covers 'in-between' services such as home-visit nursing prescribed by a doctor and nursing or medical observations at day care facilities or short-term care facilities.

Although quality of care is one of the key principles of long-term care in Korea, it is not clear how the National Health Insurance Corporation will manage and organise the quality control system. It is doubtful that a highly centralised organisation like the National Health Insurance Corporation will be able to effectively deliver local services such as screening participants in the scheme and monitoring the health condition of the beneficiaries of funds. There needs to be a focus on how to increase local governments' responsibility for quality control as well as how they might provide corresponding financial support.

Also questionable is the financial security of the long-term care insurance system. Based on Japan's experience, once the long-term care insurance system started, the demand for long-term care services unexpectedly increased. On the other hand, it is difficult to raise the premium rate to address the need for increased funds, after the inception of the insurance program. In the past, Korea has experienced financial crises in its national health insurance. In order to secure the ongoing financial viability of long-term care insurance, the proportion of the general tax revenue dedicated to this fund needs to increase.

Policy implications and conclusions

Korea is an ageing society. To cope with its ageing population, it must face many challenges, including rapidly rising health care expenditure, a weakening of family values, the economic participation of women, and so on. The introduction of long-term care insurance is, in this context, a promising action by the government. However, since Korea has little experience in delivering long-term care, the need for research into the affordability, accessibility, and quality of care of the new system is significant. The Korean Government has made a commitment to fine-tune the long-term care system to ensure continuous quality care and sustainable financing leading up to when the system begins in 2008.

Among many objectives that Korea wants to meet in addressing the needs of an ageing population, the improvement of the health of the elderly must be the ultimate goal. However, a substantial focus should also be placed on the *quality* of life of older people rather than on the quantity of life in order that older Koreans can live a longer and healthy life. The prevention of chronic diseases early in a person's life, and rehabilitation through long-term care when a person suffers a disability, are two of the key principles for healthy ageing. Some initiatives have been taken in this regard, such as the introduction of 'the Health Promotion Fund' from levying tobacco tax in 2004, as a way of paying for the health costs of smoking. This has resulted in the provision of various health promotion programs in both private and public sectors.

Apart from the health care system, pensions and retirement programs should also be strengthened. Nearly 30 per cent of the elderly still work to derive an income. If this situation does not change dramatically, it may be necessary to engage economically active seniors in long-term care not as recipients but as service managers or providers. In this way, the issues of a lack of long-term care personnel and the increasing number of elderly people with insufficient incomes can be resolved at the same time.

In conclusion, Korea is changing rapidly, both in its demographic composition and in its health care policies. In 2008, one of the biggest experiments in Korean health care history will begin with the implementation of the Elderly Care Act, reflecting Korea's ambition to overcome the challenges that lay ahead, with the ultimate goal of improving the health status of the whole population, but especially the aged.

References

Jeong K, Jo A, Oh, Y and Sunwoo D, 2001. *Caregiving conditions and welfare needs of the elderly who are eligible for long-term care.* Korea Institute for Health and Social Affairs, Seoul.

Khoo S-E & McDonald P. *The Transformation of Australia's Population, 1970-2030.* UNSW Press, Sydney, pp 77–103.

Kim J, Bae S, Park I, Gu M and Hong S, 2003. *Analysis of medical expenditure of the elderly by disease-focused on the 50 high cost diseases.* National Health Insurance Corporation, Seoul.

Leinonen R, Heikkinen E and Jylhä M, 1998. Self-rated health and self-assessed change in health in elderly men and women-a five year longitudinal study. *Social Science & Medicine*, 46, pp 591–7.

Ministry of Health and Welfare, 1999. *1998 National Health and Nutrition Survey Results.* Korea Institute for Health and Social Affairs.

Ministry of Health and Welfare, 2002. *2001 National Health and Nutrition Survey Results*, Korea Institute for Health and Social Affairs.

Ministry of Health and Welfare, unpublished. *2005 National Health and Nutrition Survey Results*, Korea Institute for Health and Social Affairs.

OECD – *see* Organisation for Economic Co-operation and Development, Paris.

Organisation for Economic Co-operation and Development, 2005. *Long-term Care for Older People.*

The Elderly Care Act 2005, Ministry of Health and Welfare.

The National Health Insurance Corporation, 2003. *Statistics of national health insurance*, Seoul.

Korea National Statistical Office, 2004. *Yearbook of the Household Survey*, Seoul.

Korea National Statistical Office, 1996. *Future Estimated Population*, Seoul.

UN – *see* United Nations.

United Nations, 2001. *World Population Ageing 1950–2050*, www.globalaging.org/ruralaging/world/ageingo.htm, accessed 20 August 2007.

10

The wider context: some key implications of generational change in Asia

Eugene Sebastian

Introduction

Asia is undergoing a tremendous change impelled by the rise of a new political and economic leadership, and the emergence of new social formations. After independence and during the Cold War, leaders of countries in the Asia Pacific region emerged from the ranks of military, bureaucratic and political elites. During this era of relative stability and fast paced economic development, at least two factors were certain: the views of the leadership and their political inclination. In the next few years this is set to change. A new generation (35–50 years old) is now coming into positions of political, economic and military influence and leadership. Within the region's social dynamics, rapid transformation driven by the growing influence of the 20- and 30-year-olds is beginning to exert political and economic influence over their country's development. They're young, cosmopolitan, mostly Western educated, globalised in their thinking and high spenders. Asia's generational transition and social transformation raises new questions about how the region will develop in the next five to 10 years and its implications for Australia. For Australia it will be increasingly important to track, understand and act on these changes as we continue to identify more strongly with the region.

As a conclusion to this book this chapter will widen the perspective beyond two key nations and explore some of the changes taking place in Asia as the geographical and social context that brings Australia and Korea together. This chapter will focus on the social and political aspects of generational change in Asia, particularly on the emergence of new leadership and the inextricably intertwined changing social formations that have emerged. There are some clear messages that can be taken from the work of the researchers from Australia and Korea whose work has been presented in the previous chapters. These messages relate primarily to challenges of generational change within the countries and some of the key social issues that have emerged, challenging both their governments and broader societies. The way these changes are addressed will rely on the stability and capacities of leaders in government throughout the Asian region, thus highlighting the importance of how the region more broadly is affected by generational change. The issues of generational change affecting the governance and political direction of the region are the same generational issues discussed in the previous chapters – the digital generation, the sandwich generation and the ageing population are making demands on leadership and government and are crucial issues for political and economic stability in the region.

Leadership in transition

In Korea, the 2002 election of outsider, President Roh Moo-hyun, marked the completion of Kim Dae Jung's presidency and the end of a political generation. Roh represented the first post-war generation politician to head the nation. He symbolised liberals, favouring economic equality and a more autonomous foreign policy, while his rival, Lee Hoi-chang, stood for the ruling political elites who tended to be traditional and conservatives in their thinking. Roh's rise, on the one hand was viewed as a victory of reform, post-cold war sentiment and anti-regionalism (Hoon Juang, 2003). Others attribute the victory also to the use of the Internet as a powerful media in mobilising a younger generation in support.

At the core of this generational shift in Korean politics is the emergence of what is dubbed the '386' generation. About 20 of President Roh's top advisers are 386ers. (Lee, 2006) The number three represents those in their late 30s; young and hungry for power and influence. The number eight represents the 1980s when they attended University during a tumultuous period in Korean history, the shift from dictatorship to democracy, and the number six represents the 1960s, when they were born during the era of rapid Korean industrialisation. They are highly educated, digitally adept, entrepreneurial and form the backbone and the policy force in Rho's administration. The 386 generation is more conspicuously cautious about embracing the dictates of the United States, especially in relation to their belligerent northern neighbour, North Korea. They are idealistically determined to root out corruption and are seeking to develop closer relations with China and Japan (Sunhyuk & Wonhyuk, 2007).

In China, the 'fourth generation' of leaders has formally assumed power. The first generation of leaders was represented by Mao Zedong, Zhou Enlai, Liu Shaoqi, leaders that started the People's Republic of China. A common characteristic of the first generation leaders is that they tended to be both political and military leaders, educated in China and involved in the Long March, Chinese Civil War and the Second Sino-Japanese War. The second generation was represented by leaders involved in the Chinese revolution but in junior roles such as Deng Xiaoping, Chen Yu, Hu Yaobang and Zhao Ziyang. Unlike the first generation many of the second generation were educated overseas. The third generation however were leaders born before the revolution, educated overseas, mostly in the Soviet Union, and were either political or military leaders. The third generation included Jiang Zemin, Li Peng, Zhu Rongji and Liu Ruihuan.

The current crop of leaders, known as the 'fourth generation' or the 'republican generation' are aged in their late 50s and early 60s, are much younger than their elders who assumed leadership positions in their late 60s and early 70s. The republican generation includes current president, Hu Jintao, Wen Jiabao, Zeng Qinhong and Wu Bangguo. Cheng Li suggests that collectively the fourth generation of leaders is less dogmatic, more capable and more diversified (2001:17). The majority of the leaders grew up during the Cultural Revolution, many acquiring their first political experience during the revolution.

> They grew up in a political environment characterised by idealism, collectivism, moralism and radicalism. They were taught to sacrifice themselves for socialism. But as time passed, their faith was eroded and their dreams shattered (2001: 18).

The fourth generation leaders, suggests Cheng Li, are more diversified than previous generations in terms of political solidarity and occupational backgrounds. Cheng Li's study of 522 high-ranking leaders in the fourth generation shows that about half of them joined the Party during the decade of the Cultural Revolution. Another 35 per cent joined the Party before, and 15 per cent joined after the Cultural Revolution. (There is roughly a 15-year span between the oldest and youngest members of the fourth generation.) Unlike the previous generation that shared strong bonding experiences such as the Long March and the Anti-Japanese War, the fourth generation of leaders lack political solidarity and a willingness to commit to the existing political system (2001: 18).

This new power cohort has shed its ideological baggage, is better educated than its predecessors and more supportive of economic and political reform. While in previous years the most important posts in China's financial system were usually occupied by Soviet-trained engineers, today's leaders are technocrats. There are more financial experts and lawyers in the fourth generation than in previous generations. At their heels are the 'fifth generation', in their 30s to 40s. Educated in elite universities in the European Union and the United States, they are reputedly liberal in their outlook and are already attaining ministerial status.

In Japan, in September 2006, 51-year-old Shinzo Abe was elected by a special session of Japan's National Diet to replace retiring Prime Minister Junichiro Koizumi. In a country where power is based on seniority and rank, Prime Minister Shinzo Abe is Japan's youngest post-World War II prime minister and the first born after the war. His ascension to power is owed largely to three factors: his family pedigree: his father served as foreign minister in the 1980s and his grandfather was prime minister in the 1950s; his hawkish position on Japan foreign policy, particularly his nationalist stance on North Korea and Japan's broader military activism in East Asia; and his youthful appeal and energy needed to reignite Japan's reform.

Under Prime Minister Abe, Japan is becoming more 'muscular in its rhetoric and posture'. Under this rising regional assertive tendency is a new generation of political leadership. A new political generation called the *Heisei* generation is now on the road to political ascension. *Heisei* is used to describe the current era name in Japan. The *Heisei*, which refers to seeking peace at home and abroad, emerged at the end of the Cold War in 1989 and after the death of Emperor Hirohito the same year. His successor, Emperor Akihito chose the name 'Heisei' to symbolise his reign. Under the *Heisei* era, a new generation of leaders emerged, who strongly supported Koizumi's reform. Kenneth Pyle observes Koizumi's unusual decision to make his cabinet appointments irrespective of factional politics and to reach policy decisions more independent of the LDP party council reflected the predilection of younger party members (Pyle, 2006: 26). Young Japanese coming to maturity in the Heisei years, adds Pyle (2006), are experiencing the kind of decisive change that gives rise to a new political generation.

The rest of Asia is not far behind this type of generational change in political leadership. In the past couple of years, Singapore has allocated key cabinet posts such as finance, defence and information technology to younger ministerial candidates. The prime ministerial succession is already in place for 2007. In Indonesia, the 'cowboys' that brought down Abdurrahman Wahid are moving into key political positions. These young and affluent players claim to hate corruption and are seen by many as the 'new hope' for dismantling the Suharto-era structures.

> The young leaders of Asia share a range of characteristics regardless of their political affiliation. They grew up in a peaceful and prosperous region and have no living memory of the Second World War and its aftermath. Ito Joichi, a young Internet entrepreneur and venture capitalist, born in 1966, wrote in 2005 on the 60th anniversary of the atomic bombings: The bombings don't really matter to me, or, for that matter, to most Japanese of my generation. My peers and I have little hatred or blame in our hearts for the Americans...My grandparents' generation remembers the suffering, but tries to forget it. My parents' generation still does not trust the military. The pacifist stance of that generation comes in great part from the mistrust of the Japanese military...For my generation, the Hiroshima and Nagasaki bombings and the war in general now represent the equivalent of a cultural 'game over' or 'reset' button.

> Through a combination of conscious policy and unconscious culture, the painful memories and images of the war have lost their context, surfacing only as twisted echoes in our subculture. The result, for better and worse, is that 60 years after Hiroshima, we dwell more on the future than the past (as cited in Pyle, 2006: 29).

They're mostly western educated, appeal to a young constituency, and are more assertive and less dedicated to the status quo. They are more concerned about the future and pay less attention to the past. They appear to be increasingly nationalistic but are in fact more assertive about their nation's self identity and the need to pursue its own interest even if it means dissenting from greater global powers.

Asia's next generation of leaders will face four defining policy challenges. They need to respond to social forces unleashed by the economic reforms of the past decade; creatively accommodate and cope with an acutely organised, complex and robust society; innovatively respond to the dilemmas of the new economy driven by technology and communications; address the needs of changing demographics, particularly the ageing of their populations and; navigate the challenges of global 'terrorism' and global economic volatility.

Social and political transformation

When discussing issues around generational changes in Asia, three themes seem to emerge: the contrast between traditionalism and modernisation stemming from the increasing global awareness of the younger generation and the consequent widening gap between the younger and older generations; the transformation in value systems and political attitudes; and a shift in consumption and the increasing influence of new technologies (Song, 2003; Beech, 2004; Marshall, 2003;
Nhu-Ngoc Ong, 2004: 1–4; Fahey, 2003: 82–5).

Tradition and modernity

Generational change across Asia has brought about a situation of contrast and confrontation between tradition and modernity. As younger generations move into positions of social, political and economic significance, a major issue they face is the role tradition has in an increasingly modern Asia (Fahey, 2003: 82–5; Nhu-Ngoc Ong, 2004:1; Song, 2003). Many Asian youth are becoming disillusioned with the older generations' inability to solve social problems and the inherent cronyism and corruption within governments. Such disillusionment widens the gap between the young and the old leading to social and political repercussions.

As mentioned above, what is interesting about Roh's propulsion to Korea's highest office is that it was driven in large part by the mobilisation of a younger generation. Young voters between the ages of 20-39 came to account for more than half of the whole electorate for the first time in South Korean history. This age group outnumbered Roh's opponent by more then 20 per cent and occupied almost half (48 per cent) of the entire vote, helping Roh secure a victory by 2.3 per cent of the vote. This so- called '20/30 generation', suggests Hoon Juang (2003), constituted the majority of 'red devils' who frenziedly rooted for their team during its 2002 World Cup victories. Half a million 'red devils' filled the squares in front of the Seoul City Hall and Gwangwhamoon every time the home team took the field. When a United States military court delivered a not guilty verdict to US soldiers who were driving vehicles that killed two Korean schoolgirls, the 20/30 generation spearheaded nationwide anti-American protests that have continued since November 2002. "Soccer fans and anti-American protesters both represent the national pride, self-determination, and self-expression of a new generation" (Hoon Jaung, 2003: 4).

The election of a political outsider in Korea seems to reflect a revolt against tradition and the elite political establishment. The preference for leadership change is driven, in part, by two important variables: the aspiration of the younger generation determined to escape from old customs and old fashioned habits in an era of fast pace economic growth; and the discontentment with the older generation's perceived 'passive and conservative actions' in dealing with social problems. In his observation of the Korean election, Ho Keun Song (2003) suggested that the youth push for Roh was merely to remove tradition and the 'gentlemen's club' in 'revolt against achievement and legacy of the old generation'. The tendency was instead to mobilise and promote what he refers to as the 'commoner-oriented sentiment in politics and society', a sentiment that emphasises human rights, equality and justice.

A similar changing attitude is occurring within the Chinese Communist Party (CCP) as a result of generational change. Freeman (2003) for example, argues that while major policy departures are unlikely, 'incremental, orderly change' has begun to take place in the hope of improving the government's ability to handle social issues. Freeman (2003) discussed the SARS (Severe Acute Respiratory Syndrome) crisis as an example of the government's failure to handle an emergency due to its reversion to traditional ways of controlling information. During the crisis, the Chinese government attempted to cover up the severity of the situation announcing that the number of cases was 1500 with only 67 fatalities. However, China's health ministry later reported that the nationwide death toll from SARS stood at 79, with 1807 confirmed cases (Gittings, 2003). The younger generation are realising the need to adopt more modern processes within government and in relation to the control and diffusion of information.

Western colonialism and numerous civil wars throughout the region have had a tremendous impact on Asian politics and social institutions. The process of modernisation has been particularly fast paced, leaving people in the region very little time to adjust (Nhu-Ngoc Ong, 2004:1). Despite the absence of wars and conflicts, Asia's younger generation has experienced transitions from a 'traditional society to a post-industrial society in a single generation' (Fahey, 2003: 82). "Unprecedented economic and technological change throughout Asia has made it difficult for Asian culture and politics to 'keep up', this having a deep impact on younger generations who are attempting to forge a sense of national and person identity" (2003: 82). As such, the question of tradition versus modernisation is particularly significant to the phenomenon of generational change.

Song (2003:5) has attempted to address the compatibility of tradition and modernity in his observations of the election of President Roh. He argues that what is occurring in Korea is a situation of 'cultural strife', a 'generational mission against the legacy of high-speed growth' through which the younger generation is trying to construct a form of 'symbolic power' for their generation. He argues that fast-paced change implemented by his generation has resulted in a younger generation that are directly opposed to fast paced change and all things associated with it (including 'traditional' processes of government) (Song, 2003:19). He states that:

> The main purpose of cultural strife is to overthrow all inheritance from authoritarian, cold war, and growth-first ideology as shackle of free imagination and uncurbed exploration to future utilizing information technology (Song, 2003:8).

Thus, while Song (2003:10–12) describes 'cultural strife' as a form of rebellion against the older generation, he also provides numerous points that legitimise the younger generation's changing attitudes to tradition and modernisation. Song's analysis is useful as it highlights one reaction to generational change from within Asia, thus providing insight into how generational change in politics is having an impact on the region.

At another level, Hutzler (2002) discusses the influence of globalisation and Westernisation on generational change in China, posing the question of the extent to which traditional Chinese institutions and values are compatible with Western values and institutions. Hutzler suggests that a prominent issue facing the new generation of leaders in China will be how they handle dealing with the West, and govern 'China's increasingly complex and close relationship with the rest of the world'. Similarly, some observers look at the possibility of a 'hybrid' solution as younger generations become more globally aware –the notion that Asian youth wish to remain 'a little bit East, a little bit West' when looking at issues of society and politics (Hill, 2003; Nhu-Ngoc Ong, 2004: 1).

What indeed seems to be the consensus is that generational change in Asia is resulting in the development of a younger generation that is much more globally aware, and much more sensitive to the possibility of merging modern Western ways of doing things with more traditional customs and institutions. However, there are many questions surrounding the implications of tradition and modernity and the widening distance between generations for the phenomenon of generational change in Asia. 'Will the next generation lead their countries toward political pluralism or increased nationalism? Will growing anti-Americanism among the young in Korea and Japan give rise to a more politically powerful China globally? How will young peoples' dissatisfaction with authoritarian governments as well as corrupt political parties in the new democracies play out?' Generational change (particularly in terms of the relationship between tradition and modernity) as it affects international economic and security architecture, is so significant that it is relevant to ask what impact this will have on Australia. Will it be easier to do business if Asia is more open to Western economic structures? As it is still uncertain how the changing role of tradition and modernity within Asia will affect Australia, this area requires further research.

Transformations in value systems and political attitudes

Fewsmith (2002) suggests that generational succession is always important, because different generations have different formative experiences, different expectations about the world, and different types of training on which to draw when dealing with problems. Generational change in Asia is characterised by a significant alteration of value systems that are reflected in the political attitudes of the younger generation. The process of democratisation and globalisation taking place throughout the region are having a vast impact on how the younger generation view themselves. Asian youth are becoming more aware of Asia's growing relationship with the rest of the world. An increasingly high percentage of the younger generation are benefiting from the opportunity of studying overseas in Western institutions. They are becoming more open-minded and adaptive, post-material, increasingly individualistic and much more concerned with issues of social welfare (Marshall, 2003; Nhu-Ngoc Ong, 2004: 1). In Japan for example, the transforming value system is represented by young people who are less driven by the all-consuming work ethic characteristic of their parents' fears of poverty. They are much more concerned with personal fulfilment and share distaste for hierarchy and convention in the workplace (Marshall, 2003).

Recent discussions on generational change in the region examined the development of post-materialism, focusing on the situation of 'cultural strife' in South Korea. Song (2003:10–12) for example, describes rapid economic development and social differentiation as major contributing factors to changing value systems, as political freedom and market competition have become central to the younger generation. Song (2003:11) highlights the desire to shift from 'hard politics' to 'soft politics', as the younger generation is increasingly concerned with issues of human rights, peace, gender equality, and environmental protection. The election of President Roh is symbolic of this change in values, reflecting the shift of policy weight to distribution and social welfare for lower classes:

> It is apparent that the Roh government's utmost goal is to promote social integration and remedy social displacement by improving distributive justice and fulfilling essential aspects of post-material values (Song, 2003:15).

Fahey (2003) also discusses the influence of changing value systems on political attitudes, describing the younger generation's political agenda as being concerned with challenges to obligation and patriarchy within the family and workplace; engagement with and responses to globalisation; and tendencies towards nationalism, anti-Americanism and democracy (Fahey, 2003: 85).

A study conducted by The Centre for Strategic and International Studies in 2002 on the implications for the United States of generational change in Japan provides a very detailed investigation of the phenomenon of generational change. According to the study, young leaders in Japan share common characteristics regardless of their political affiliation: they grew up in a relatively peaceful and prosperous period, having no living memory of the Second World War or its aftermath. They are arguably more assertive and less committed to the status quo. They are more concerned with the future and less concerned with the past. They are increasingly nationalistic, attempting to forge a Japanese identity and greater international role. They are, however, unable to clearly articulate Japanese national interests and goals, or provide a clear blueprint for political and economic reform. In contrast to previous generations, they do not feel burdened by Japanese history, believing instead that Japan should come to terms with its past and move forward (The Centre for Strategic and International Studies, 2002: 3).

According to Fahey, the Post-Tiananmen square generation in China has become more nationalistic, expressing dissatisfaction with their government for not protecting them against international humiliation (2003: 92). Post World War II tensions still exist within China in younger generations, however they are manifested differently than in previous generations (Fahey, 2003: 84; Sutter, 2002). According to Sutter, current negativity in the Sino-Japanese relationship has developed due to 'strong and often growing areas of mutual interest' (Sutter, 2002). Relative weakening of Japanese economic performance and political leadership has 'coincided' with an increase in Chinese power and influence in Asian affairs. Within China, these tensions have evolved from Chinese leaders' focus on Japan as having victimised China in the past, thus linking it to the recent promotion of nationalism within China (Sutter, 2002).

Another issue related to changing value systems stems from the increasing role of international education. According to current literature, a common experience shared by the younger generation across Asia is that of overseas education in Western institutions (Fahey, 2003: 83; Sebastian, 2003; Song, 2003; *The Economist*, 2004). As a result, this generation has been increasingly exposed to Western economic and political procedures and social institutions. A significant question that must be asked is what impact this will have on Australia. Does culture in terms of international business become less important or less of a barrier?

Technology and consumption

Figure 10.1. Internet users by world region

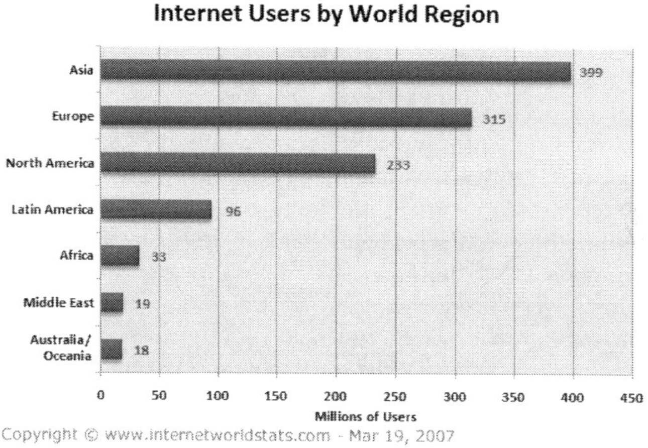

Source: Internet World Stats 2007

The role of technology and consumption is the third significant theme in a discussion about generational change in Asia. In the latest data on Internet usage, Asia has the highest number of Internet users with nearly 400 million users compared with Europe with 315 million and North America with 233 million users. Throughout Asia, more people are gaining access to the Internet and are buying mobile phones. This is resulting in a revolution in the way people (in particular younger generations) communicate and relate to their society, as these new technologies are providing a new space for interaction (Fahey 2003; McMahon, 2004; Song, 2003). As previously discussed, Asian youth are very much engaged with politics (Fahey, 2003: 83) and are now beginning to challenge issues in a new public sphere – cyberspace. The Internet and mobile phones (text messaging) are increasingly being used to discuss social and political issues and even to influence elections. New technologies make communication between large numbers of people across long distances relatively easy and fast, providing greater freedom of information (Song, 2003). Asia's new generation has been described as 'technologically savvy' due to their propensity for this new technology. Approximately two thirds of the South Korean population utilise the Internet, and across Asia in general, new jobs in digital technology are being created, making the ideal of lifelong employment old-fashioned.

Fahey (2003) in her study, 'Generational Change and Cyberpolitics in Asia' provides a detailed introduction to the profusion of new technology in Asia and the impact this is having on society and politics. Fahey proposes that new technology, the Internet (especially chat rooms) and text messaging are providing a new social forum that is separate from both government regulation and the older generation. Younger generations are using new technology to express opinions, launch campaigns, report on events, et cetera (Fahey 2003: 105). Fahey sees this new public sphere are being central to generational change as for the first time transnational communication is easily accessible, thus altering the dimensions and structure of public space (2003: 90–91). Fahey describes the Internet as significant as it involves "costless reproduction, is decentralised, and [allows] instantaneous dissemination of information" and, as such, has revolutionised political activity throughout Asia (2003: 104). As stated above, the election of President Roh, exemplifies the use of new technology and political participation. Song argues that the Internet provides a 'generational voice' for younger generations, stating that the use of the Internet and text messaging to assist with the election of Roh was aimed at 'mobilising generational solidarity' (2003:9). Internet demonstrations in South Korea were so powerful that they assisted with the fall of the 'gentleman's club' from the centre of politics and society. The use of text messaging, 'blogging', online campaign audio/videos are increasingly becoming a norm during elections. Similarly, the Internet and text messaging have been used in Indonesia and China to challenge various points of authority and to affect political activity. Whether the Internet creates a new form of democracy in Asia remains to be seen. There have been numerous attempts by governments to cordon off and limit the use of the Internet in political mobilisation.

The rapid infiltration and use of new technology has also resulted in a transformation within consumerism in Asia. This in itself is significant as it illustrates the impact of younger generations on the larger economic sphere. Younger generations are gaining increasingly wider access to new technology and as a result desire greater control over what they buy and the services they use. As recently reported in *The Korea Times* (2005) there is a new generation of consumers, labelled 'prosumers' due to their increasing tendency to be involved in the consumption process. This reflects an analysis of the changing behaviour of young consumers in Korea, calling them 'generation C ers' due to their creativity and changing consumption habits (*The Korea Times*, 2005). There is apparently a current shift away from passive, straightforward consumption within younger generations to customisation or even co-production of products (*The Korea Times*, 2005). As such, generation 'C' has 'transformed marketing into a two-way conversation' between corporations and consumers, as consumption becomes all about 'you' (*The Korea Times*, 2005). This transformation of consumerism will have an increasing impact on the economic sphere as newer technologies become available. An important question arises for Australia: how will this transformation affect Australia in terms of Australia's import and export markets with Asia?

While the protrusion of new technologies and the changing nature of consumerism have resulted in increased creativity, individualism and greater communication across Asia, there are also numerous negative implications within this facet of generational change. At present, access to the Internet and mobile phones is not equal throughout Asia or even within nations, this 'digital divide' being cause by differences in 'income, age and gender' (Fahey, 2003:97–8). Between different areas in China there is a formidable wealth-divide (Hill, 2003) resulting in certain groups being excluded from the benefits of new technology and social formations (McMahon, 2004). Similarly, there is a limited penetration of new technology within Southeast Asia, and as such the use of the Internet and mobile phone for political purposes is restricted to the urban elite (Fahey, 2003: 95). In Malaysia, while most youth enjoy a high level of affluence and tend to be 'technologically savvy', there is a large sector of rural youth whose basic needs are not being met (AASSREC Conference, 2003: 1). In addition, the Internet and mobile phones are largely inaccessible to older generations throughout the region, resulting in a division between younger and older generations. Here, Fahey acknowledges the potential social problems posed by the digital divide (2003: 98). If, as Fahey suggests, new technology (such as the Internet and mobile phones) becomes the major form of political engagement and democracy development (assuming democracy is the chosen path), groups excluded from access to new technologies may feel even further disenfranchised (2003: 98). The impact of the digital divide thus requires further investigation in terms of its social, political and economic repercussions, as well as its implications for Australia-Asia relations.

Conclusion

As a rounding off of the range of issues raised in this book on the impact of generational change in Australia and Korea, this chapter has mapped out a number of key discussions involved in a region in transition. It has also highlighted a number of research gaps in studies on the impact of generational change in Asia. For example, there is little to no research on how 'generational change' has affected the foreign policy of Asian countries. More research also needs to be conducted on how 'generational change in Asia' will affect Australia in terms of economic, political, and cultural relations. Further, more empirical data needs to be developed on trends in changes in attitudes to political and economic relations, and social problems that can be used to back up current conclusions. Finally, there is currently a significant imbalance in the amount of information on China and Japan compared to any other country, demonstrating a great need for research to be conducted on the causes and consequences of generational change in other Asian countries.

Within a specific context, this book examines the social policy challenges emerging as a result of demographic shifts taking place in Australia and Korea. It specifically considers some of the social and demographic changes in both countries with a particular focus on addressing their demographic make-up and the common challenges of decreasing fertility rates, the ageing population and the need for improved health care systems. It also addresses the issue of technology and its impact on the digital generation – those born between 1979 and 1994. This generation is the beneficiary of the economic boom of the late 80s and 90s and has been brought up in an era of excessive mobile phone use and of ubiquitous, fast and cheap access to Internet. This book has also examined the generation sandwiched between ageing parents who need care and their own children. 'Chewed at both ends', they struggle to support ageing parents and pay for the education of their children. There is indeed a need to rethink child care and family support schemes and the traditional role of women as homemaker. Finally, the book addresses how society will cope with the changing health and financial needs of an ageing population. How will economies increase productivity so that shrinking workforces can maintain expanding pool of retirees? What policy changes need to be made to adjust to these changing demographics?

Current debates and discussions on social policy tend to compare Australia with the United States and the United Kingdom. This book attempts to redress that imbalance by offering new perspectives of Australian society through a comparison with South Korea, in light of the importance of the relationship between the two nations. There still remain a great number of issues related to generational change that need to be examined hopefully this book has made that step towards addressing some of them.

References

Bates Gill J, Morrison S and Thompson D, 2004. *Defusing China's time bomb: Sustaining the momentum of China's HIV/AIDS response* [online], 13–18 April. Washington DC: Centre for Strategic and International Studies. Available from: http://www.csis.org/media/csis/pubs/040413_china_aids.pdf [accessed 6 January 2007].

Beech H, 2004. The new radicals, Time, January 26. Available from: http://www.time.com/time/magazine/article/0,9171,582466-2,00.html [accessed 14 December 2006].

Fahey S, 2005, Generational change and cyberpolitics in Asia, in Fay Gale and Stephanie Fahey (eds.), Youth in transition: The challenges of generational change in Asia, Proceedings of the 15th Biennial General Conference, Association of Asian Social Science Research Council & Academy of Social Science Australia, Canberra, pp 89–107.

Gale F & Fahey S (eds.), 2005. Youth in transition: The challenges of generational change in Asia, Proceedings of the 15th Biennial General Conference, Association of Asian Social Science Research Council & Academy of Social Science Australia, Canberra.

Fewsmith J, 2002. Generational Transition in China. *The Washington Quarterly*, 25 (4), p 23.

Freeman D, 2003. China's new leaders face challenge. *EurAsia*, 7 (4).

Gittings J, 2003. China says SARS outbreak is 10 times worse than admitted, The Guardian. Available from: http://www.guardian.co.uk/sars/story/0,13036,940372,00.html [accessed 14 November 2006].

Hills S, 2003. Challenges for the fourth generation, Business Asia, April. Available from: http://findarticles.com/p/

articles/mi_m0BJT/is_3_11/ai_102451313 [accessed 27 October 2006].

Hennock M, 2002. Inside China's 'Me' generation. *BBC News* [online], 6 November. Available from: http://news.bbc.uk/2/hi/business/2403661.stm [accessed 15 July 2006].

Hoon Jaung, 2003. President Roh Moo-hyun and the new politics of South Korea. *Asia Society* [online], February. http://www.asiasociety.org/publications/update_korea2.html [accessed 5 December 2006].

Hutzler C, 2002. China's new generation of leaders keep a low profile as they push for reforms [online]. Available from: http://tin.le.org/vault/wireless/china.new.generation.html [accessed 21 October 2007].

In-Yong Rhee, 2003. The Korean election shows a shift in media power, Nileman Reports, International Journalism, Spring 2003. Available from:http://findarticles.com/p/articles/mi_hb3330/is_200303/ai_n8049115 [accessed 3 December 2006]

Jackson Richard, 2005. *Preparing for China's aging challenge* [online], 1 May. Washington DC: Centre for Strategic and International Studies. Available from: http://www.csis.org/component/option,com_csis_pubs/task,view/id,885/type,1/ [accessed 15 November 2006].

Kim S and Lim W, 2007. How to deal with South Korea. *The Washington Quarterly*, 30 (2), pp 71–82.

Li Cheng, 2001. China's political succession: Four misconceptions in the West, Asia Program Special Report, The Wilson Centre, No. 96, June, pp17–23. Available from: http://wwics.si.edu/topics/pubs/asiarpt_096.pdf [accessed 5 January 2007].

Lee B J, 2006. South Korea: Too much activism, *Newsweek International Edition* [online], November 27. Available from: http://www.msnbc.msn.com/id/15790420/site/newsweek/ [accessed 15 January 2007].

Marshall A, 2003. Can the Class of '89 fix Japan? *Time* [online], 16 June. Available from: http://time.com/time/asia/2003/class89/story.html on 10/06/03] [accessed 15 January 2007].

McMahon D, 2004. Taming China's Nationalist Tiger. *Business Asia*, April. Available from: http://findarticles.com/p/articles/mi_m0BJT/is_2_11/ai_99987078 [accessed 15 June 2006].

Nathan A J and Gilley B, 2002. The Fourth Generation. *The Australian Financial Review*, 11 October, pp 1–2, 11.

Nhu-Ngoc Ong, 2004. Changes in Attitudes toward Democracy among Asian Generations. *Conference on Citizens, Democracy and Markets around the Pacific Rim*, March 19–20. Honolulu, Center for the Study of Democracy, UC Irvine, the University of Missouri.

Pyle K B, 2006. Abe Shinzo and Japan's change of course, *NBR Analysis*, 17 (4), p 26.

Sebastian E, 2003. Asia's next generation – point of view. Business Asia, August. Available from: http://findarticles.com/p/articles/mi_m0BJT/is_7_11/ai_109402858 [accessed 9 March 2004].

Song H K, 2003. Politics, generation and the making of new leadership in South Korea. *Paper presented at conference Korea Re-examined: New Society, New Politics, New Economy?* Research Institute for Asia and the Pacific, University of Sydney, Sydney, 23 February, pp 1–15 unpublished.

Sutter R, 2002. China and Japan: trouble ahead? The Washington Quarterly, 25:4, pp 37-49.

The Centre for Strategic and International Studies, 2002. Generational Change in Japan: its implications for US-Japan Relations, August. Available from: http://www.csis.org/media/csis/pubs/genchangejapan.pdf [accessed 15 March 2006].

The Economist, 2004. The end of tycoons. *The Economist* [online], 27 April. http://findarticles.com/p/articles/mi_hb5037/is_200004/ai_n18276363 [accessed 25 March 2005].

Trendwatching.com, 2005. http://www.trendwatching.com/about/inmedia/articles/generation_c/digital_generation_leads_new_m.html [accessed 25 March 2005].

Author unknown, 2005. Digital Generation Leads New Marketing Patterns. *The Korea Times*, 25 January.

Author biographies

Mubarak Ali is a Lecturer at the School of Social Administration and Social Work at Flinders University in Adelaide. His research interests include the experience of adolescents while interacting through the Internet, and the social and psychological impacts of chat-rooms on adolescents. He has completed one of the first Australian studies into the psychological impact of the Internet in teenagers aged between 15 and 17. Currently he is conducting research entitled, "A study on risk-taking behaviours of adolescents in the Internet and their implications on child safety in Australia".

Deborah Brennan is an Associate Professor in the Department of Government and International Relations at the University of Sydney. Her teaching and research interests are in comparative social policy, the history and politics of welfare states and the restructuring of welfare states. She has particular expertise in the areas of families and work, community service provision, taxation and social security and has published extensively on these topics. Dr Brennan's current research projects include a major study of work and family policies in Australia, the USA and Europe. Her publications include *The Politics of Australian Childcare: From Philanthropy to Feminism, Caring for Australia's Children: Political and Industrial Issues in Childcare Provision and Towards a National Childcare Policy*. She has written articles on gender and representation, civil society and social policy and has contributed to the *Cambridge Encyclopaedia of Australia* and the *Oxford Companion to Australian Feminism*.

Gil-Soo Han is an Associate Professor and currently Head of Arts at Monash University Malaysia. He has researched and published widely in the areas of sociology of religion, health, migrants and Korean studies. His most recent work includes *Healthcare Reform and Interest Groups: Catalysts and Barriers in Rural Australia* (with Evans and Madison, 2006) and papers in *Journal of Sociology, Ethnicity & Health, International Journal for the Study of the Christian Church*. His current research includes *Bridging the Digital Divide in Rural Agricultural & Fishing Communities in Malaysia*.

Eun-jeong Kang is a research fellow at the Korea Institute for Health and Social Affairs, a government-funded research institute in Korea. Her research interest is in health promotion, measurement of health status including health-related quality of life. She has been actively engaged in national health promotion policy development and was also responsible for the Health Interview Survey of the 2005 National Health and Nutrition Survey that was the major data source of the national health promotion policy.

Her recent research papers have dealt with summary measures of population health, gender difference in the prevalence of disabilities in activities of daily living, and population segmentation by healthy lifestyle.

Hal Kendig is Research Professor of Ageing and Health in the Faculty of Health Sciences at the University of Sydney, and National Convenor of the ARC/NHMRC Research Network in Ageing Well. Professor Kendig recently served on the 'Promoting Healthy Ageing' Working Party for the Prime Minister's Science, Innovation, and Engineering Committee (PMSIEC), the Building Ageing Research Capacities (BARC) Committee of the Department of Health and Ageing, and the United Nations Expert Group for a Global Research Agenda on Ageing. He served as Dean of the Faculty of Health Sciences from 1998 to 2005, and as Director of the Lincoln Gerontology Centre at La Trobe University, a Key Centre of the Australian Research Council, from 1989 to 1998. His book, "Who Should Care for the Elderly?" (2000), co-edited with William Liu, was awarded the Outstanding Book Award by the Australasian Journal on Ageing.

Ik Ki Kim is Professor of Sociology at Dongguk University, Seoul. He participated in the 'Expert Group Meeting on Policy Responses to Population Ageing and Population Decline' hosted by the United Nations Secretariat in 2000 and is part of the editorial board for the Hallym International Journal of Ageing. He has written extensively on changing demographics, fertility and the ageing population in Korea, Japan and China. Professor Kim was a Visiting Scholar at the Institute of Gerontology at the University of Michigan and Sophia University in Tokyo, Japan. In 2005, he took up a position as Visiting Scholar at Renmin University of China in Beijing, PRC.

Jeong-Hee Kim is a research Professor at the Korean Women's Institute, Ewha Women's University in Seoul. Her major publications include The *Present and Prospective Influence of Bio-feminist Politics* (2005), *Globalisation and Women's Civil Rights in Korea* (2002, co-author) and *Mother at the Same Height of Her Child's Eyes, Child Growing to Be One's Dream* (2000). Professor Kim also served as vice-director for the Cooperative Childcare Research Institute from 1998–1999.

Heejin Lee is an Associate Professor at the Graduate School of International Studies, Yonsei University, Korea. Before joining GSIS, Yonsei, he was a faculty member at the University of Melbourne and Brunel University, UK. Dr Lee has written extensively on the impact of broadband in South Korea and time and IT. He is currently working on IT for development. His work has been published in a variety of journals including *The Information Society, Time & Society, Information & Management*, the *Journal of Information Technology*. He is an associate editor of *European Journal of Information Systems*.

Peter McDonald is Professor of Demography and Director of the Australian Demographic and Social Research Institute at the Australian National University. He is Vice President (2006-2009) and President-elect (1010-2013) of the International Union for the Scientific Study of Population. Prior to his present appointment he was Head of Research at the Australian Institute of Family Studies for 11 years. Peter's recent work has focused on the implications of low fertility for population futures and the related policy concerns.

Sangjo Oh is Associate Professor at the Department of Internet Business, Dongyang Technical College, Korea. He earned his master and doctoral degrees from Seoul National University. His research interests are on the role of social constructs in the implementation, diffusion, and success of information systems. He has published his research in many of journals, including the Journal of Information Technology, Journal of Strategic Information Systems, and INFO.

Ruth Phillips is a senior lecturer in the Social Work and Social Policy program in the Faculty of Education and Social Work at the University of Sydney. She teaches across postgraduate, research and undergraduate programs on subjects as diverse as ageing and global social policy. Her primary areas of research are social policy and third sector studies. She has published extensively in journals in these fields. She has a particular interest in the Asia pacific region and in Korea more specifically due to a lengthy involvement in conducting seminars for visiting social work and welfare professional from Korea.

Eugene Sebastian has experience in project design, management, evaluation and monitoring. He has been instrumental in implementing technical assistance projects for the United Nations Development Program (UNDP), UNICEF, Asian Development Bank and AusAID. Having had a brief stint serving as program developer for a multinational training firm, he is also experienced in developing corporate training activities and cross-cultural training courses. Eugene is a doctoral candidate with the Department of Government and International Relations, University of Sydney. He holds a BA (Hons) from Flinders University in South Australia and speaks fluent Bahasa Malaysia.

Don Stammer has been a member of the Australia-Korea Foundation since it was formed in 1992 and its chairman since 2001. Don has a master's degree from the University of New England and a doctorate from the Australian National University. He has had a long-term interest in Asian economies and in conservation. Don's first career was as an academic. Over the 1970s, he held senior positions in the Reserve Bank. In 1981, Don joined the investment bank Bain & Company (subsequently Deutsche Bank Australia) where he was, for many years, director of investment strategy. Subsequently, he was a director of the ING group in Australia. He is a non-executive company director.

Index

Printed in Dunstable, United Kingdom

91222484R00130